Well Said Intro
Pronunciation for Clear Communication

SECOND EDITION

Linda Grant and Eve Einselen Yu

NATIONAL GEOGRAPHIC
L E A R N I N G

Australia · Brazil · Mexico · Singapore · United Kingdom · United States

NATIONAL GEOGRAPHIC
LEARNING

***Well Said Intro: Pronunciation for Clear Communication*, Second Edition**
Linda Grant and Eve Einselen Yu

Publisher: Sherrise Roehr

Executive Editor: Laura Le Dréan

Associate Development Editor:
Jennifer Williams-Rapa

Media Researcher: Leila Hishmeh

Senior Technology Product Manager:
Scott Rule

Director of Global Marketing: Ian Martin

Product Marketing Manager: Dalia Bravo

Sr. Director, ELT & World Languages:
Michael Burggren

Production Manager: Daisy Sosa

Content Project Manager: Beth Houston

Senior Print Buyer: Mary Beth Hennebury

Composition: MPS Limited

Cover/Text Design: Brenda Carmichael

Art Director: Brenda Carmichael

Cover Image: Patrick Aventurier/Getty
Images & Daniel Buren; Excentrique(s) travail
in situ in MONUMENTA 2012, Grand-Palais
Paris. ©Daniel Buren + ADAGP Paris.

For product information and technology assistance, contact us at
Cengage Learning Customer & Sales Support, cengage.com/contact

For permission to use material from this text or product,
submit all requests online at **cengage.com/permissions**
Further permissions questions can be emailed to
permissionrequest@cengage.com

Student Edition:
ISBN: 978-1-305-64142-6

National Geographic Learning
20 Channel Center Street
Boston, MA 02210
USA

National Geographic Learning, a Cengage Learning Company, has a mission
to bring the world to the classroom and the classroom to life. With our English
language programs, students learn about their world by experiencing it. Through
our partnerships with National Geographic and TED Talks, they develop the
language and skills they need to be successful global citizens and leaders.

Locate your local office at **international.cengage.com/region**

Visit National Geographic Learning online at **NGL.Cengage.com/ELT**
Visit our corporate website at **www.cengage.com**

Printed in China
Print Number: 04   Print Year: 2019

Contents

Appendices

Index   I1

Scope and Sequence

CHAPTER	OBJECTIVES	RULES AND PRACTICE	COMMUNICATIVE PRACTICE	PRONUNCIATION LOG
PART I Introduction to Pronunciation				
1 **Your Pronunciation Needs and Goals** *pages 2–7*	You will: • learn how you can improve your pronunciation. • think about how pronunciation affects communication. • set personal goals for the course.			
2 **Syllables** *pages 8–13*	You will learn: • to identify a syllable. • to identify the number of syllables in a word. • to use a dictionary to identify syllable stress.			
3 **Vowel and Consonant Sounds** *pages 14–21*	You will learn: • vowel sounds and their common symbols. • consonant sounds and their common symbols. • vowel sounds in stressed and unstressed syllables. • a useful sound–spelling rule for vowels.			
PART II Word Endings				
4 **Final Consonant Sounds** *pages 23–31*	You will learn: • the importance of pronouncing final consonant sounds clearly. • the pronunciation of final voiceless and voiced consonant sounds. • the pronunciation of vowel sounds before final voiceless and voiced consonant sounds.	4.1 Final Consonant Sounds 4.2 Final Consonant Sounds and Vowel Length	What? I can't hear you!	• Record and submit a voicemail message. • Self-monitor for final consonant sounds.

Scope and Sequence

CHAPTER	OBJECTIVES	RULES AND PRACTICE	COMMUNICATIVE PRACTICE	PRONUNCIATION LOG
5 **The -s Ending** *pages 32–39*	You will learn: • the importance of pronouncing -s endings clearly. • the grammatical forms that take -s endings. • the different pronunciations of the -s ending.	**5.1** Final -s Sounds **5.2** Sound and Spelling: -es	Describe Your Dream Job	• Record and submit job descriptions. • Self-monitor for the -s ending.
6 **The -ed Ending** *pages 40–46*	You will learn: • the importance of pronouncing -ed endings clearly. • the grammatical forms that take -ed endings. • the different pronunciations of the -ed ending.	**6.1** Final -ed Sounds	Life Stories	• Record and submit a story. • Self-monitor for the -ed ending.
PART III Word Stress				
7 **Stress in Numbers, Nouns, and Verbs** *pages 48–58*	You will learn: • to make syllables in words sound stressed. • to use simple guidelines to determine the stress in numbers, nouns, and verbs.	**7.1** Stress in Numbers **7.2** Stress in Two-Syllable Nouns **7.3** Stress in Two-Syllable Verbs **7.4** Stress in Two-Syllable Noun and Verb Pairs **7.5** Stress in Compound Nouns	Troubles with Technology	• Record and submit an announcement. • Self-monitor for stress in numbers, nouns, and verbs.
8 **Stress in Words with Suffixes** *pages 59–66*	You will learn: • to make syllables in words sound stressed. • to predict stressed syllables in words with common suffixes.	**8.1** Word Stress: Suffixes -ion and -ity **8.2** Word Stress: Suffixes -ic and -ical **8.3** Word Stress: Suffix -ian	Qualities of a Successful Employee	• Record and submit a text about sleep positions. • Self-monitor for stress in words with suffixes.

Scope and Sequence

CHAPTER	OBJECTIVES	RULES AND PRACTICE	COMMUNICATIVE PRACTICE	PRONUNCIATION LOG
PART IV Sentences: Rhythm and Connected Speech				
9 **Rhythm: Stressed Words** *pages 68–76*	You will learn: • about English rhythm in phrases and sentences. • which words are stressed. • why words are stressed.	9.1 Content Words and Sentence Stress 9.2 Structure Words and Sentence Stress	Voicemail	• Record and submit limericks. • Self-monitor for rhythm of stressed words.
10 **Rhythm: Reduced Words** *pages 77–85*	You will learn: • that structure words are usually reduced. • what reduced words sound like. • how reduced words are weakened.	10.1 Reducing Structure Words 10.2 Dropping /h/ in Structure Words 10.3 *Can* versus *Can't*	Finish the Conversation	• Record and submit proverbs. • Self-monitor for rhythm of reduced words.
11 **Connected Speech** *pages 86–93*	You will learn more about: • how to link or connect words. • how sounds get changed or lost when we connect words.	11.1 Linking: Final Consonant to Beginning Vowel 11.2 Linking: Final Consonant to Same Consonant 11.3 Linking and Sound Change: /t/ Between Vowels (*a lot of* = *alodda*) 11.4 Linking and Sound Change: Final /d/ + /y/	Good Manners	• Record and submit idioms. • Self-monitor for connected speech.
PART V Discourse: Focus, Intonation, and Thought Groups				
12 **Focus Words** *pages 95–103*	You will learn: • what a focus word is. • how focus words are pronounced. • which words are focus words, and why.	12.1 Focus Words 12.2 Hearing the Focus Word 12.3 Special Focus: New Information 12.4 Special Focus: Answering *Wh-*Questions 12.5 Special Focus: Making Corrections 12.6 Special Focus: Contrasting Information	Check Your Facts	• Record and submit statements. • Self-monitor for focus words.

Scope and Sequence

Symbols in *Well Said Intro*

Vowel and Consonant Symbols

Vowel Sounds and Symbols

Key Word	Well Said
1. **e**at, d**ee**p	/i^y/
2. **i**t, d**i**p	/ɪ/
3. l**a**te, p**ai**n	/e^y/
4. l**e**t, p**e**n	/ɛ/
5. c**a**t, f**a**n	/æ/
6. b**ir**d, t**ur**n	/ɜr/
7. c**u**p, s**u**ffer	/ʌ/
about, symb**o**l	/ə/
8. h**o**t, st**o**p	/ɑ/
9. t**oo**, n**ew**	/u^w/
10. g**oo**d, c**ou**ld	/ʊ/
11. r**oa**d, n**o**te	/o^w/
12. l**aw**, w**a**lk	/ɔ/
13. f**i**ne, r**i**ce	/ay/
14. **ou**t, n**ow**	/aw/
15. b**oy**, j**oi**n	/ɔy/

Consonant Sounds and Symbols

Key Word	Well Said
1. **p**ie	/p/
2. **b**oy	/b/
3. **t**en	/t/
4. **d**ay	/d/
5. **k**ey	/k/
6. **g**o	/g/
7. **f**ine	/f/
8. **v**an	/v/
9. **th**ink	/θ/
10. **th**ey	/ð/
11. **s**ee	/s/
12. **z**oo	/z/
13. **sh**oe	/ʃ/
14. mea**s**ure	/ʒ/
15. **ch**oose	/tʃ/
16. **j**ob	/dʒ/
17. **m**y	/m/
18. **n**o	/n/
19. si**ng**	/ŋ/
20. **l**et	/l/
21. **r**ed	/r/
22. **w**e	/w/
23. **y**es	/y/
24. **h**ome	/h/

Symbols for Stress, Rhythm, and Intonation

WORD STRESS	In a word, the syllable with the main stress is in **bold**.	au to **ma** tic
	Sometimes the syllable with the main stress has a large circle above it.	au tö ma tïc
RHYTHM	In a phrase or sentence, the stressed words (or syllables) are in **bold**.	I **found** my **wal**let.
	Sometimes the stressed words (or syllables) have large circles above them.	I found my wallet.
LINKING	A link mark shows that the final sound of one word connects to the beginning of the next word.	Should we sit down or stand up?
FOCUS	The most important word in a phrase or sentence, the focus word (or the stressed syllable of the focus word), is in bold *and* underlined.	A: The movie's at **eight**. B: Let's eat be**fore** the movie.
INTONATION	An arrow points down if the final pitch falls. An arrow points up if the final pitch rises.	He's a cook. ↘ Is he a cook? ↗
THOUGHT GROUPS	The end of a phrase or thought group is marked with a slash.	My older sister / who lives in Michigan / just had a baby!

To the Instructor

Welcome to the second edition of *Well Said Intro: Pronunciation for Clear Communication*. *Well Said Intro* is designed to improve the pronunciation and communication skills of students from all language backgrounds. The important features of pronunciation are introduced here at a beginning to low-intermediate level. For an intermediate to advanced presentation, see *Well Said,* which introduces and spirals these pronunciation features at a higher level.

The *Well Said* series was written for general English language learners but is especially useful for students aiming to succeed in academic, business, scientific, and professional settings. The two levels are flexible and can be used for classroom, lab, blended, or online study. They are also well suited for one-on-one tutorials or for self-study, especially in conjunction with the online workbook.

Parts I–V focus on the "music" of the language—syllables, stress, rhythm, thought groups, and intonation. These features are often problematic for students from all language backgrounds.

Part VI provides supplemental practice for selected consonant and vowel sounds, features that are more likely to vary depending on your students' first languages. See the instructor's manual (provided for free on the course website) for information about students from a variety of language backgrounds.

The text also provides these distinctive features:

- a clear course plan for teachers who lack a background in pronunciation teaching
- integration of pronunciation with listening and speaking
- progression from structured practice to relevant communicative practice
- multi-sensory practice to help students internalize skills
- active learner involvement in monitoring and self-evaluation

We hope this text serves as an effective guide for improving your students' pronunciation, and we appreciate feedback from users of *Well Said Intro*. If you have suggestions, comments, or questions, please forward them to us through the publisher.

Linda Grant and Eve Einselen Yu

New to This Edition

New to this edition of *Well Said* are the following:

- updates to content that reflect **current research** in second language pronunciation learning, especially as it relates to features of pronunciation most likely to interfere with intelligibility.
- a **re-organized** chapter structure that will allow teachers and students to advance through the material more efficiently and productively.
- an **all-new online workbook** providing added hours of listening and pronunciation practice, enabling students to work at their own pace and on their own time, and allowing teachers the ability to see (and hear) their students' progress.

- **student and teacher companion websites** with easy access to the complete student book audio program. Teachers also have access to the *Well Said Intro Instructor's Manual*, which includes audio scripts, answer keys, suggestions for using the text, information about pronunciation teaching and learning, and resources regarding common pronunciation problems of students from various language backgrounds. Go to **NGL. Cengage.com/wellsaid**

Organization of the Text

Moving in order through each chapter will result in a coherent presentation. At key points in the text, a "Choose Your Path" note alerts instructors to options that allow for customization based on students' needs.

Except for the introductory chapters, all chapters follow a similar format.

- **WARM UP:** Each chapter begins with a contextualized, fun, and often interactive activity that introduces students to the pronunciation features to come. Student awareness is gently raised before they move on to noticing the features.

- **NOTICE:** The chapter continues with exercises to help students perceive the target pronunciation feature and to help students build skills for peer- and self-monitoring.

- **RULES & PRACTICE:** Next, students discover pronunciation rules and patterns. The structured exercises help students gain control of pronunciation features before applying them in more challenging communicative contexts.

- **COMMUNICATIVE PRACTICE:** After the learners practice each feature in a controlled manner, they move on to a contextualized communicative practice. This section includes interactive practice that recycles the rules in the chapter as they occur in a variety of everyday situations. The Communicative Practice section guides learners as they bridge the gap between a focus on accuracy and a focus on meaning. It provides the opportunity for students to test their hypotheses, make mistakes, and get teacher feedback. Furthermore, it enables students to observe how pronunciation concepts affect meaning in communication.

- **PRONUNCIATION LOG:** The final segment in each chapter recycles target pronunciation features in an individual speaking activity. Students listen to and record themselves saying things such as quotes, stories, poems, and voicemail messages. Then they monitor themselves prior to receiving feedback from their instructor.

- Tips, practice strategies, and useful information about pronunciation are included throughout the text in segments called "Tip" and "Did You Know."

Acknowledgments

The author and publisher would like to thank the following reviewers:

Kelsey Anderson, Pacific University; **Britta Burton,** Mission College; **Rachel De Santo,** Hillsborough Community College; **Margaret Eomurian,** Houston Community College Central; **Joyce Gatto,** College of Lake County; **Liz Holloway,** Kansas City Community College; **Amy Loewen,** Laney College; **Mary Lukasik,** Houston Community College; **Joanna Luper,** Liberty University; **Barbara Luther,** Irvine Valley College; **Catherine Moore,** California State University, Fullerton; **Lukas Murphy,** Westchester Community College; **Donna Obenda,** University of North Texas, Denton; **Barbara Raifsnider,** San Diego Community College District; **Kristina Rigden,** University of California, Riverside; **Nancy Sell,** University of New Hampshire; **Rebecca Smith,** Syracuse University; **Lucy Sutherland,** Boston University; **Ellen Yaniv,** CELOP/Boston University; **Stan Zehr,** Fairfax County Public Schools.

From the Authors

My greatest thanks go to Eve Einselen Yu, my valued co-author, for bringing a fresh voice and new vision to this edition. I am also indebted to the publisher and the editorial team at National Geographic Learning/Cengage, for their continuing faith in the *Well Said* series. Finally, sincere thanks to the scholars whose research is beginning to inform pronunciation texts like this.

Linda Grant

First, I'd like to thank Linda Grant for the wonderful opportunity to work with her on the second edition of *Well Said Intro*. Next, I thank Laura Le Dréan and the team at National Geographic Learning at Cengage Learning for their work and efforts to make the product a success, including our organized, kind, and *very* patient editor, Kasia McNabb. I'd also like to thank my husband Ritchie for his love, support, and regular willingness to serve as a guinea pig. Lastly, I'd like to thank my orange tabbies, Huck and George, for keeping me company and for letting me know each day when it was time to stop working.

Eve Einselen Yu

Credits

Cover: ©Patrick Aventurier/Getty Images. Daniel Buren; Excentrique(s) travail in situ in MONUMENTA 2012, Grand-Palais Paris. ©Daniel Buren + ADAGP Paris

Photo and Cartoons: xiv Erin Korff **(right)**, **01** Getty Images Entertainment/Getty Images, **08** Mike Flanagan/Cartoonstock.com, **22** Yadid Levy/Anzenberger/Redux, **34** Royston-Robertson-/CartoonStock Ltd, **39** EduWales/Alamy Stock Photo, **46** SelectStock/Vetta/Getty Images, **47** Mads Nissen/Panos Pictures, **65** Tom Cheney/The New Yorker Collection 2002/Cartoonbank.com, **67** Luca Locatelli/Institute Artist, **71** Bacall, Aaron/CartoonStock Ltd, **72** Dynamic Graphics/liquidlibrary/Getty Images, **75** Alias Ching/Shutterstock.com, **78** Corey Pandolph/Condé Nast Collection, **85** Roy Nixon/CartoonStock Ltd, **92** Wilbur-Dawbarn/CartoonStock Ltd, **94** The Asahi Shimbun/Getty Images, **96** © 2015 Randy Glasbergen, **109** McPherson, John/CartoonStock Ltd, **117** Ken Kochey, National Geographic Creative, **126** © 2009 Hilary B. Price Distributed by King Features Syndicate, Inc., **131** Patrick Forde/CartoonStock Ltd, **139** W. B Park/CartoonStock Ltd, **143** Guy & Rodd/CartoonStock Ltd, **152** Pablo Stanley, **157** RGJ -Richard Jolley/CartoonStock Ltd, **161** Andrew Toos/CartoonStock Ltd, **173** Nate Fakes/CartoonStock Ltd, **180** Harley Schwadron/CartoonStock Ltd.

To the Student

Many of you can read, write, and understand North American English well, but your pronunciation may make clear and effective communication challenging. The *Well Said Intro* program will help you improve your pronunciation so that you can communicate confidently and be understood with ease.

This program focuses on common pronunciation problems for all learners of English. The rules and practice are presented at a beginning to low-intermediate level of English. Once you are comfortable with the concepts, the next level (*Well Said,* 4th edition) will help you to practice them at a higher level. Repeated practice with both listening and speaking will help you to internalize the rules and speak naturally.

In the classroom, we encourage you to collaborate with classmates as both a speaker and a listener. As a listener, you will hear examples of clear and unclear pronunciation from your classmates. This will help you learn what makes speech easy or hard to understand, so know that this time is not wasted. It will also help you understand and correct issues with *your own* pronunciation.

Here are a few more points to consider:

- Mistakes are a natural and necessary part of learning, so don't be afraid to make them.

- You don't need to speak with 100 percent accuracy. A better goal is to work on the aspects of your pronunciation that make clear communication difficult.

- Your attitude is important in pronunciation improvement. You will make more progress if you are strongly motivated to improve.

- You will learn more quickly if you listen to and speak English outside of the classroom.

We hope this edition of *Well Said Intro* helps you in your efforts to speak English clearly.

Linda Grant and Eve Einselen Yu

Linda Grant

Eve Einselen Yu

PART I Introduction to Pronunciation

Visitors taking a break from the International Contemporary Art Fair at the Grand Palais, Paris

1

CHAPTER 1 Your Pronunciation Needs and Goals

OBJECTIVES
In this chapter, you will:
* learn how you can improve your pronunciation.
* think about how pronunciation affects communication.
* set personal goals for the course.

SUMMARY
What are your pronunciation needs? What are your goals? This chapter will help you and your teacher assess the features of pronunciation that are most challenging for you. It will also help you set individual goals for learning pronunciation.

Warm Up

EXERCISE 1

A Work with a partner. Ask your partner questions. Write your partner's answers in the chart.

Interview Questions	Notes
1. What's your name?	
2. What languages do you speak?	
3. Where are you from?	
4. What do you study? (*or*) What kind of work do you do?	
5. What are your interests or hobbies?	
6. What are three adjectives that describe you?	

B Introduce your partner to your class.

> My name is _____ , and I'd like to introduce _____ .

C As you listen to your classmates, take notes in your notebook. Write at least one thing that you heard about each student.

TIP ▼ **What should you do if someone doesn't understand you?**

Don't worry. It happens all the time. Just repeat your words and speak a little more slowly. Stop and pause briefly after each idea.

What are your interests or hobbies?

I love hiking and swimming.

I'm sorry? Could you repeat that, please?

Sure. . . . I love hiking . . . and swimming.

EXERCISE 2   Read and answer these questions. Then discuss your answers in a group.

1. Were your classmates sometimes difficult to understand in Exercise 1? Why? Check ✔ the three most common reasons.

_____ speed   _____ vowel sounds   _____ word stress

_____ loudness   _____ consonant sounds   _____ rhythm or beat

2. What features of pronunciation do you feel are the most important for you to practice? Why?

DID YOU KNOW ?   Have you ever seen a food pyramid? For a healthy diet, you have to eat from all the food groups. Pronunciation is like that, too. Consonant and vowel sounds are important ingredients, but alone they cannot help you speak clearly. Features like stress, rhythm, and intonation are important, too. To successfully communicate in English, focus on all pronunciation features in the pyramid.

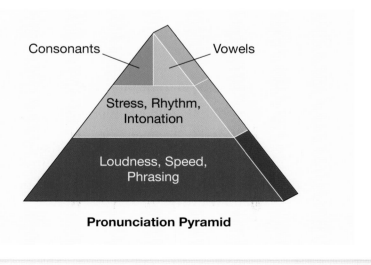

Pronunciation Pyramid

Complete one or more of the following exercises. Your teacher will use the Pronunciation Needs Form on page 5 to tell you which features are important for you to study.

EXERCISE 3 **A** Read the paragraph silently. If you do not understand something, ask your teacher or use a dictionary. Then practice reading the paragraph aloud.

Why are you studying pronunciation?

What are your pronunciation goals? Do you need to sound like a native speaker? Do you have to lose your accent completely? How clear does your speech have to be?

Before you set goals, ask yourself a few questions. When do you need to speak English the most? For example, do you use the telephone at work? If so, your pronunciation needs to be very clear. Do you want to have casual conversations with friends or classmates? Then your speech can be more relaxed.

You do not need perfect pronunciation. You can speak with an accent and still be clear.

In this course, you will learn the most useful pronunciation features. You will also learn that improving pronunciation takes time, patience[1], and motivation[2]. In fact, the more motivated you are, the more progress you will make. This book will help you track your progress so that you can hear your improvement.

[1]patience (n) calmness, ability to do something without becoming angry or upset
[2]motivation (n) desire and energy to do something

B When you are ready, record yourself reading the paragraph. Read as naturally as possible. Submit the recording to your teacher.

EXERCISE 4 **A** Choose one of these prompts. Think about your answers.

1. Talk about your last trip or vacation. Where did you go? What did you do? How was it?
2. Tell about one of your family members (mother, father, sister, brother, . . .). Tell his or her name, age, and interests or occupation.
3. When or where is it most important for you to speak English? List a few places and tell why.

B Record your answers to the prompt you chose. Submit the recording to your teacher.

Pronunciation Needs Form

Write your name and the date. Your teacher will complete this form.

Name: _____ Date: _____

Pronunciation Features

Part	Feature	1 Little/No control	2 Some control	3 Good control	Examples
I	**Syllables** (Ch. 2, 3)	1	2	3	
	Vowel Sounds (Ch. 3; Part VI: Vowel Sounds 1–7)	1	2	3	
	Consonant Sounds (Ch. 3; Part VI: Consonant Sounds 8–17)	1	2	3	
II	**Word Endings** (Ch. 4, 5, 6)	1	2	3	
III	**Word Stress** (Ch. 7, 8)	1	2	3	
IV	**Rhythm: Stressed Words** (Ch. 9)	1	2	3	
	Rhythm: Reduced Words (Ch. 10)	1	2	3	
	Connected Speech (Ch. 11)	1	2	3	
V	**Focus Words** (Ch. 12)	1	2	3	
	Final Intonation (Ch. 13)	1	2	3	
	Thought Groups (Ch. 14)	1	2	3	

Delivery

Loudness: ☐ too soft ☐ good ☐ too loud

Speed: ☐ too slow ☐ good ☐ too fast

Body Language (note eye contact and other physical movements):

_____

Strengths:

1. _____

2. _____

3. _____

Needs:

1. _____

2. _____

3. _____

EXERCISE 5   **A** Work in a group. Discuss your answers to these questions. Choose one person to take notes and another to report to the class.

1. Have you ever listened to people who do not speak your native language well? What makes them hard to understand? What makes them easy to understand?
2. What makes native speakers of English hard to understand? What makes them easy to understand?

B Write two words or phrases that are difficult for you to say in English. Why do you think they are difficult?

Difficult Word/Phrase: _____

Why is it difficult? _____

Difficult Word/Phrase: _____

Why is it difficult? _____

___

TIP ▼ A Pronunciation Log

It is a good idea to keep a record of words and phrases that are difficult for you to say. Then when you see your teacher or friends, you can ask them for help. See Appendix A, page A1 for a place to record new words and phrases.

___

EXERCISE 6   **A** In what situations do you want to improve your English? Check ✓ the three most important situations for you.

_____ talking on the telephone	_____ speaking at meetings
_____ casual conversations with friends	_____ teaching in English
_____ talking with coworkers	_____ giving short reports
_____ asking/answering questions in class	_____ participating in discussions
_____ talking with non-native speakers of English	_____ other: _____

B In a small group, make a list of the most common answers from part **A**. Then report them to the class.

EXERCISE 7 **A** Read the Pronunciation Levels below. Circle your current pronunciation level. Then set a goal for the level you want to reach by the end of this course. Check ✓ your goal.

Pronunciation Levels

____ **Level 1: Very low**
Listeners understand only occasional words.

____ **Level 2: Low**
Very frequent errors create a lot of difficulty with understanding.

____ **Level 3: Fair**
Frequent errors create some difficulty with understanding.

____ **Level 4: Good**
Some errors create confusion but no major difficulties with understanding.

____ **Level 5: Great**
You have an accent, but it rarely causes a misunderstanding.

____ **Level 6: Native-like**
You sound like a native speaker of English.

B Look again at the information your teacher provided on the Pronunciation Needs Form on page 5. Write the three most important pronunciation features for you to learn.

1. _____

2. _____

3. _____

CHAPTER 2 Syllables

OBJECTIVES

In this chapter, you will learn:

- to identify a syllable.
- to identify the number of syllables in a word.
- to use a dictionary to identify syllable stress.

SUMMARY

Syllables are the building blocks of English words. Each syllable in a word has one vowel sound and usually one or more consonant sounds.

How Many Beats?

EXERCISE 1   **A** 🔊 Words have one, two, three, or more syllables or beats. Listen. CD 1; Track 2

One Syllable	Two Syllables	Three Syllables
tea	ta • co	ba • na • na
quit	qui • et	qui • et • ly

B 🔊 Listen again. Say the words with the speaker. CD 1; Track 2

EXERCISE 2 **A** 🔊 The word *cookie* has two syllables: coo-kie. Listen and say the words with the speaker. With your finger, tap each syllable as you say it. CD 1; Track 3

One Syllable	Two Syllables	Three Syllables
tap ↓ cook rain	tap tap ↓ ↓ coo • kie rain • drop	tap tap tap ↓ ↓ ↓ de • li • cious um • brel • la

B Look at the words in part **A**. How many vowel sounds are in each syllable? _____

C Write the number of consonant sounds in the underlined syllables.

1. <u>cook</u> and <u>rain</u>: ___2___

2. <u>de</u> <u>li</u> cious: _____

3. rain <u>drop</u> and um <u>brel</u> la: _____

TIP ▼ Use a Dictionary

Most dictionaries separate syllables with dots or dashes. The pronunciation of the word is shown between the slashes (//). The word *umbrella* has three spoken syllables. The word *business* has two.

um•brel•la /ʌm ˈbrɛ lə/   **busi•ness** /ˈbɪz nəs/

EXERCISE 3 **A** 🔊 Listen to each pair of words. Is the number of syllables the same or different? Check ✓ the correct box. CD 1; Track 4

			Same	Different
1.	black	blue	✓	☐
2.	box	boxes	☐	✓
3.	do	does	☐	☐
4.	act	actor	☐	☐
5.	quiet	quite	☐	☐
6.	bank	basic	☐	☐
7.	look	looked	☐	☐
8.	decide	decided	☐	☐
9.	beginner	introduce	☐	☐
10.	Korea	vanilla	☐	☐

B 🔊 Compare your answers with your class. Then listen again and check. CD 1; Track 4

EXERCISE 4 **A** 🔊 Listen. Check ✓ the word you hear. CD 1; Track 5

One Syllable	Two Syllables	Two Syllables	Three Syllables
1. ✓ cook	___ cookie	7. ___ center	___ senator
2. ___ planned	___ planet	8. ___ present	___ president
3. ___ say	___ essay	9. ___ explained	___ explain it
4. ___ sit	___ city	10. ___ omit	___ omitted
5. ___ stopped	___ stop it	11. ___ tasted	___ tasted it
6. ___ small	___ some mall	12. ___ Erik	___ Erika

B 🔊 Check your answers with your class. Then listen to the speaker say each pair of words in part **A**. Tap for each syllable. CD 1; Track 6

EXERCISE 5 **A** 🔊 Here are the 20 most beautiful words in the English language according to one survey. Listen. Then circle the five words you like the best. CD 1; Track 7

Most Beautiful English Words

1. mother	6. fantastic	11. peace	16. cherish
2. passion	7. destiny	12. blossom	17. enthusiasm
3. smile	8. freedom	13. sunshine	18. hope
4. love	9. liberty	14. sweetheart	19. grace
5. eternity	10. tranquility	15. gorgeous	20. rainbow

B Write the five words you circled in part **A**. Then write the number of syllables in each word. Check your dictionary if you are not sure.

Words   **Syllables**

1. _____   _____

2. _____   _____

3. _____   _____

4. _____   _____

5. _____   _____

C Work in a group. Think of five English words that your group does NOT like the sound of. Write the words and the number of syllables in each.

Words   **Syllables**

1. _____   _____

2. _____   _____

3. _____   _____

4. _____   _____

5. _____   _____

D Share your group's most disliked word with the class.

TIP ▼ Do not omit or add syllables if you want your meaning to be clear.

If you omit a syllable, you may change the meaning of the sentence.

We need-ed it.	4 syllables = past
We need it.	3 syllables = present

If you add a syllable, the meaning may also change.

Where's the stu-dent cen-ter?	6 syllables = place
Where's the stu-dent se-na-tor?	7 syllables = person

EXERCISE 6 **A** Work with a partner. Write the number of syllables or beats in each word or phrase.

1. __3__ potato   7. _____ forty

2. _____ desk   8. _____ needed

3. _____ menu   9. _____ needed it

4. _____ clock   10. _____ stopped

5. _____ magazine   11. _____ stopped it

6. _____ tomato   12. _____ chocolate

B 🔊 Listen to each word or phrase and check your answers. **CD 1; Track 8**

Which Syllable Is the Strongest?

EXERCISE 7 **A** 🔊 In words with two or more syllables, one syllable is stronger than the others. The strongest syllable has the main or primary stress. Listen to these words. **CD 1; Track 9**

Two Syllables	Three Syllables	Four Syllables
tu na	**re** ci pe	a vo **ca** do
ca **reer**	suc **cess** ful	e **co** no my

B 🔊 Listen again and tap the bold syllables more strongly as you repeat them. **CD 1; Track 10**

EXERCISE 8 **A** 🔊 You will hear each word two times. Circle the strongest (or stressed) syllable. **CD 1; Track 11**

1. ex (plain)

2. Ja pan

3. Chi na

4. un der stand

5. pre sent (n)

6. pre sent (v)

B 🔊 Now listen and say each word two times with the speaker. **CD 1; Track 11**

DID YOU KNOW ?

Most dictionaries put a mark (') before the syllable with the main or primary stress. Sometimes one word has more than one stress pattern.

For example, the first syllable has primary stress when *present* is a noun (n).

↓

(n) **pre•sent** /ˈprɛ zənt/   I received a **pre**sent on my birthday.

The second syllable has primary stress when *present* is a verb (v).

↓

(v) **pre•sent** /prɪ ˈzɛnt/   They will pre**sent** a certificate at graduation.

You will learn more about word stress in Part III.

EXERCISE 9　**A**　Work with a partner. Guess which syllable has primary stress. Circle your answer. Then check your dictionary and mark the primary stress with '.

Guess the primary stress	Check your dictionary
1. (cof) fee	'cof fee
2. po lice	po lice
3. fi nal	fi nal
4. pro mise	pro mise
5. a bi li ty	a bi li ty
6. pi a no	pi a no

B　🔊 Listen and repeat each word. **CD 1; Track 12**

TIP ▼ Pay attention to the primary stress.

In the dictionary, words with three or more syllables sometimes have three levels of stress.

1. /'/ main or primary stress　　　　　　　　ˌap pli 'ca tion
2. /ˌ/ light or secondary stress　　　　　　　ˌap pli 'ca tion
3. no stress　　　　　　　　　　　　　　　　ˌap pli 'ca tion

Pay special attention to the syllable with primary stress.

EXERCISE 10　**A**　Write five more words that are difficult for you to say. You may use words from Chapter 1, Exercise 5 on page 6. Look up the words in your dictionary. Mark the syllable with primary stress. Then write a sentence using the word.

1. _____des 'sert_____　　　　_____I love to eat ice cream for dessert._____

2. _____　　　　_____

3. _____　　　　_____

4. _____　　　　_____

5. _____　　　　_____

6. _____　　　　_____

B　Report your words and sentences to a small group.

3 **Vowel and Consonant Sounds**

OBJECTIVES

In this chapter, you will learn:
- vowel sounds and their common symbols.
- consonant sounds and their common symbols.
- vowel sounds in stressed and unstressed syllables.
- a useful sound-spelling rule for vowels.

SUMMARY

Words in English may not always sound the way they are written. For example, sometimes two words have different spellings but the same pronunciation (e.g., *there, their*). And sometimes two words have the same spelling but different pronunciations (e.g., *tear*, a drop of water from the eye; or *tear*, to rip apart). This chapter introduces symbols for the consonant and vowel sounds in North American English. It also introduces the relationship between vowel sounds and stress in words.

Spelling and Sounds

In English, when you see a letter or letters in a word, you might not know the pronunciation. This is why dictionaries use special symbols for pronunciation. For example, the word *thought* has seven letters but only three symbols or sounds.

7 letters	3 symbols or sounds
↓	↓
thought	/θɑt/

EXERCISE 1 **A** Read the pairs of words out loud. Are they pronounced the same? Check ✓ *Same* or *Different*.

			Same	Different
1.	son	sun	☑	☐
2.	pool	pull	☐	☑
3.	wear	where	☐	☐
4.	won	one	☐	☐
5.	throw	through	☐	☐
6.	threw	through	☐	☐
7.	clothes	close (v.)	☐	☐
8.	sea	see	☐	☐
9.	loose	lose	☐	☐
10.	wood	would	☐	☐

B 🔊 Compare your answers with your class. Then listen and check your answers.
CD 1; Track 13

Vowel Sounds and Symbols

Some words have the same vowel letters but different vowel sounds.

m<u>a</u>p /æ/   f<u>a</u>ther /ɑ/   <u>a</u>bout /ə/

Some words have different vowel letters but the same vowel sound.

h<u>ey</u> /eʸ/   d<u>ay</u> /eʸ/   <u>ei</u>ght /eʸ/

Each vowel sound has a symbol. These symbols help you learn the pronunciation of new words.

EXERCISE 2   **A**   Look up each key word in your dictionary. Write the pronunciation symbol for the underlined vowel sound.

Pronunciation Guide: Vowel Sounds and Symbols

Key Word	Well Said Intro	Newbury House Dictionary	Your Dictionary's Symbol
1. h<u>e</u>	/iʸ/	/i/	
2. h<u>i</u>t	/ɪ/	/ɪ/	
3. m<u>ay</u>	/eʸ/	/eɪ/	
4. g<u>e</u>t	/ɛ/	/ɛ/	
5. c<u>a</u>t	/æ/	/æ/	
6. b<u>ir</u>d	/ɜr/	/ɜr/	
7. c<u>u</u>p*	/ʌ/	/ʌ/	
<u>a</u>bout	/ə/	/ə/	
8. h<u>o</u>t, f<u>a</u>ther	/ɑ/	/ɑ/	
9. t<u>oo</u>	/uʷ/	/u/	
10. g<u>oo</u>d	/ʊ/	/ʊ/	
11. kn<u>ow</u>	/oʷ/	/oʊ/	
12. l<u>aw</u>	/ɔ/	/ɔ/	
Diphthongs			
13. r<u>i</u>ce	/ay/	/aɪ/	
14. n<u>ow</u>	/aw/	/aʊ/	
15. b<u>oy</u>	/ɔy/	/ɔɪ/	

* The vowel sound/symbol in *cup* is used in stressed words and syllables; the vowel sound/symbol in <u>a</u>bout is used in unstressed syllables.

B   🔊 Listen and repeat the key word for each vowel sound in part **A**. CD 1; Track 14

A Find the words below in your dictionary. Write the symbol for each underlined vowel sound. Then write your own word with the same vowel sound. Underline the sound.

Word	Symbol	Your Word
1. <u>e</u>gg	/ɛ/	h<u>ea</u>lthy
2. w<u>ee</u>k		
3. c<u>ow</u>		
4. s<u>e</u>nd		
5. p<u>u</u>t		
6. f<u>a</u>ther		
7. s<u>i</u>ck		
8. b<u>oo</u>t		
9. l<u>au</u>gh		
10. s<u>oa</u>p		
11. l<u>o</u>ve		
12. r<u>ai</u>lroad		

B 🔊 Listen and repeat each word in part **A**. Check your words with your class or in a dictionary. **CD 1; Track 15**

Consonant Sounds and Symbols

Like vowels, consonants can also have more than one pronunciation. These words have the same first letter but different first sounds:

<u>c</u>ar /k/   <u>c</u>ell phone /s/   <u>g</u>ood /g/   <u>g</u>iant /dʒ/

These words have different first letters but the same first sounds:

<u>g</u>iant /dʒ/   <u>j</u>uice /dʒ/   <u>s</u>end /s/   <u>c</u>ity /s/

Most consonant symbols look like alphabet letters.

/b/   /d/   /v/   /g/   /z/   /l/   /r/   /m/   /n/   /w/
/p/   /t/   /f/   /k/   /s/   /h/

Some consonant symbols do not look like alphabet letters.

/θ/ <u>th</u>ink   /ð/ <u>th</u>ey   /ʃ/ <u>sh</u>oe   /ʒ/ trea<u>s</u>ure   /tʃ/ <u>ch</u>oose   /dʒ/ <u>j</u>ob   /ŋ/ si<u>ng</u>

EXERCISE 4

A Look up each key word in your dictionary. Write the pronunciation symbol for the underlined consonant sound.

Pronunciation Guide: Consonant Sounds and Symbols

Key Word	Well Said Intro	Newbury House Dictionary	Your Dictionary's Symbol
1. pie	/p/	/p/	
2. boy	/b/	/b/	
3. ten	/t/	/t/	
4. day	/d/	/d/	
5. key	/k/	/k/	
6. go	/g/	/g/	
7. fine	/f/	/f/	
8. van	/v/	/v/	
9. think	/θ/	/θ/	
10. they	/ð/	/ð/	
11. see	/s/	/s/	
12. zoo	/z/	/z/	
13. shoe	/ʃ/	/ʃ/	
14. measure	/ʒ/	/ʒ/	
15. choose	/tʃ/	/tʃ/	
16. job	/dʒ/	/dʒ/	
17. my	/m/	/m/	
18. no	/n/	/n/	
19. sing	/ŋ/	/ŋ/	
20. let	/l/	/l/	
21. red	/r/	/r/	
22. we	/w/	/w/	
23. yes	/y/	/y/	
24. home	/h/	/h/	

B 🔊 Listen and repeat the key word for each consonant sound in part **A**.
CD 1; Track 16

EXERCISE 5 **A** Find the words below in your dictionary. Write the symbol for each underlined consonant sound. Then write your own word with the same consonant sound. Underline the sound.

Word	Symbol	Your Word
1. <u>sh</u>are	/ʃ/	wi<u>sh</u>
2. ba<u>th</u>		
3. na<u>t</u>ure		
4. lau<u>gh</u>		
5. fa<u>th</u>er		
6. ma<u>ch</u>ine		
7. wi<u>ng</u>		
8. u<u>s</u>ual		
9. <u>j</u>uice		
10. pa<u>g</u>e		

B 🔊 Listen and repeat each word in part **A**. Check your words with your class or in a dictionary. **CD 1; Track 17**

TIP ▼ Record Key Words

Keep a personal list of words that are difficult for you to say. Use the form in Appendix A, on page A1, to record the words. Here are words from one student's list:

Personal Key Word List

Word	Pronunciation	Typical Phrase
1. democratic	/ˌdɛ mə ˈkræ tɪk/	a democratic government
2. asthma	/ˈæz mə/	an asthma attack

EXERCISE 6 **A** These are some popular countries to visit. Which country begins with each sound? Write the name of the country next to its first sound.

Japan	China	Canada	~~Poland~~
Thailand	Switzerland	Mexico	Greece
United States	Spain	France	Russia

1. /p/ _Poland_

2. /k/ _____

3. /t/ _____

4. /tʃ/ _____

5. /y/ _____

6. /dʒ/ _____

B Name the country you would most like to visit. _____

C Does it begin with a consonant sound? If so, what sound? /_____ / Share your answers with your class.

EXERCISE 7 **A** 🔊 These are some popular first names. Listen and repeat them. CD 1; Track 18

Female		Male	
Charlotte	Martha	Charles	Joshua
Chloe	~~Phoebe~~	Chris	Max
Daisy	Shelly	David	Richard
Julie	Susan	~~Frank~~	Theo
Georgia	Zoe	James	Thomas

B Which names begin with each sound below? Write the names next to the sounds.

1. /f/ _Phoebe, Frank_

2. /t/ _____

3. /z/ _____

4. /tʃ/ _____

5. /dʒ/ _____

6. /ʃ/ _____

7. /θ/ _____

8. /k/ _____

C Compare your answers in part **B** with a partner.

Vowel Sounds and Stress

The most important vowel sound in a word is the vowel sound in the stressed syllable. This vowel sound should be fully pronounced.

Vowels in unstressed syllables are usually pronounced with the schwa /ə/ sound. The schwa sounds like "uh." Your lips are slightly open and your mouth is relaxed.

🔊 Listen to these words. Notice the stressed and unstressed vowel sounds. CD 1; Track 19

banana /bə 'næ nə/   Thomas /'tɑ məs/   Lisa /'liʸ sə/

EXERCISE 8   **A** Write the vowel sound in the stressed (**bold**) syllable.

1. be**gin**   / ɪ /   4. **ta**ble   / /

2. con**fuse** / /   5. No**vem**ber   / /

3. Ja**pan**   / /   6. four**teen**   / /

B 🔊 Check your answers with your class. Then listen and repeat the words. Make the stressed vowels full and clear. CD 1; Track 20

EXERCISE 9   **A** 🔊 Listen. Circle the unstressed syllables that have a schwa vowel sound. CD 1; Track 21

1. (de)ve(lop)   4. pos si ble

2. oc cur   5. com pare

3. a lone   6. tra di tion

B 🔊 Check your answers with your class. Then listen again and repeat each word. Remember that the schwa is a relaxed sound. CD 1; Track 22

Be more like the schwa. It never gets stressed.

Two-Vowel Rule

When you see two vowels in a one-syllable word, the first vowel is often pronounced like the letter name. The second vowel is silent.

ra<u>i</u>n	n<u>a</u>m<u>e</u>	=	A /e^y/
m<u>ea</u>t	f<u>ee</u>l	=	E /i^y/
p<u>ie</u>	m<u>i</u>n<u>e</u>	=	I /ay/
b<u>oa</u>t	h<u>o</u>m<u>e</u>	=	O /o^w/
<u>u</u>s<u>e</u>	bl<u>ue</u>	=	U /u^w/

EXERCISE 10 **A** 🔊 Write each phrase under the correct vowel sound. Then listen and check your answers. **CD 1; Track 23**

~~late date~~	true blue	slow boat	bike ride
arrive alive	same page	fruit juice	cream cheese
clean jeans	those coats	green tea	nice smile

A /e^y/	E /i^y/	I /ay/	O /o^w/	U /u^w/
late date				

B 🔊 Listen to the answers to part **A** again and repeat the phrases in each column. **CD 1; Track 24**

📍 CHOOSE YOUR PATH

- To learn how to make the vowel sounds, turn to Vowel Sounds 1, page 118.
- To learn how to make the consonant sounds, turn to Consonant Sounds 8, page 144.
- For fun practice with vowel sounds and spelling, turn to Vowel Sounds 2, page 125.
- For fun practice with consonant sounds and spelling, turn to Consonant Sounds 9, page 150.

PART II Word Endings

Diners eat at Cicciolina restaurant, Cuzco, Peru.

4 **Final Consonant Sounds**

OBJECTIVES

In this chapter, you will learn:

* the importance of pronouncing final consonant sounds clearly.
* the pronunciation of final voiceless and voiced consonant sounds.
* the pronunciation of vowel sounds before final voiceless and voiced consonant sounds.

SUMMARY

English words often end in one or more consonant sounds (*car*, *card*, *cards*). Words with final consonants are less common in many other languages. Therefore, it can be difficult for English learners to hear or say consonant sounds at the ends of words. This chapter will explain how final consonant sounds affect meaning and how to say them clearly and correctly.

Warm Up

EXERCISE 1 **A** 🔊 Listen to the voicemail message. Circle the words you hear. CD 1; Track 25

"This is a message for (1. Jay / Jake). My name is (2. Lee / Leif), and I'm calling about the science club meeting. It's tonight at 7:00 in (3. Room A / Room 8) of Smith Hall. Please bring your lab (4. coat / code). Also, we plan to talk about this year's fair. We need to figure out the (5. price / prize). All ideas are welcome! Thank you, and see you later. Oh, one more thing, if you can, please bring chips or another snack."

B Check your answers with your class. Tell your classmates any words you misunderstood.

EXERCISE 2 **A** 🔊 Listen. The speaker will say sentence *a* or *b*. Circle the one you hear.
CD 1; Track 26

1. a. There's Joe.

b. There's Joan. ⟵ (b circled)

2. a. Here's the tray.

b. Here's the train.

3. a. Go to Gate 811.

b. Go to Gate A-11.

4. a. Can you dry?

b. Can you drive?

5. a. The cap was expensive.

b. The cab was expensive.

6. a. This is my right.

b. This is my ride.

B 🔊 Check your answers with your class. Then listen to both sentences in each pair from part **A**. Do you notice a difference? CD 1; Track 27

Rules and Practice

Final Consonant Sounds

If you omit final consonant sounds:

• you might change the meaning. For example, *pain* may sound like *pay*.

A: *Is your pay bad?*
B: *My pay? Why do you want to know?*
A: *No, is your **pain** bad?*

• you might not make sense. For example, *nine men* may sound like *ni-men*.

A: *Ni-men called about the job.*
B: *Who's Nimen?*
A: *No, **nine men** called. Many people are interested in the job.*

RULE 4.1 If you want to be clear, do not omit final consonant sounds.

EXERCISE 3   **A** 🔊 Listen to the sentences. Check ✓ *Correct* if you hear the underlined consonant sound. Check *Incorrect* if you do not. CD 1; Track 28

	Correct	Incorrect
1. Take the ti<u>m</u>e off.	☐	☑
2. Did you sa<u>v</u>e money?	☐	☐
3. It's noo<u>n</u> in my country.	☐	☐
4. What's the da<u>t</u>e of the party?	☐	☐
5. Kee<u>p</u> up the good work.	☐	☐
6. Can you sea<u>t</u> us together?	☐	☐

B 🔊 Check your answers with your class. Then listen to the correct sentences from part **A**. Say them with the speaker. CD 1; Track 29

📍 CHOOSE YOUR PATH

• For practice with specific consonant sounds, turn to Consonant Sounds 10–17, pages 153–180.
• For more practice with final consonant sounds, continue with the chapter.

TIP ▼ Linking Final Consonants to Words Beginning with a Vowel

When a word with a final consonant is followed by a word beginning with a vowel, link the consonant to the vowel in the next word. The final consonant will be easier to say, and your speech will sound more natural. Listen. **CD 1; Track 30**

time off	→	ti- moff	keep up	→	kee- pup
date of	→	da- tof*	at a	→	a- ta*

*When linking a final /t/ to a vowel, the /t/ sound often sounds like a fast "d."
For example: *date of* sounds like "*da-dəv*" and *at a* sounds like "*a-də*."

EXERCISE 4

A 📢 Listen to the speaker say sentence *a* or *b*. Check ✓ the matching response. **CD 1; Track 31**

1. a. Can the hostess <u>see us</u>?
   b. Can the hostess <u>seat us</u>?
   ____ No, we should move closer to her.
   ✓ No, there isn't a free table yet.

2. a. Should I take the <u>tie off</u>?
   b. Should I take the <u>time off</u>?
   ____ Yes, it doesn't match your shirt.
   ____ Yes, you need a vacation.

3. a. Does he <u>say anything</u>?
   b. Does he <u>save anything</u>?
   ____ No, he's very quiet.
   ____ No, he doesn't have any money.

4. a. Your red <u>boat is</u> nice!
   b. Your red <u>bow is</u> nice!
   ____ Thanks! Do you want to go for a ride?
   ____ Thanks! It's made of silk.

5. a. What's the <u>date of</u> the meeting?
   b. What's the <u>day of</u> the meeting?
   ____ May 14th.
   ____ Tuesday.

6. a. I'm afraid I don't like my <u>tea</u>.
   b. I'm afraid I don't like my <u>team</u>.
   ____ Would you prefer coffee?
   ____ Please try to work with everyone.

B Check your answers with your class.

C Work with a partner. Look again at the sentences in part **A**. Student A, say sentence *a* or *b*. Student B, say the matching response. Remember to practice linking consonants with vowels.

> Can the hostess seat us?

> No, there isn't a free table yet.

CHOOSE YOUR PATH

- For information on voiceless and voiced consonants, turn to Consonant Sounds 8, page 144.
- For practice with final consonant sounds and vowel length, continue with the chapter.

Final Consonant Sounds and Vowel Length

◀) Listen to each word pair. How are the vowel sounds different in these word pairs? **CD 1; Track 32**

Voiceless	Voiced
rope	robe
coat	code
pick	pig
leaf	leave
price	prize

RULE 4.2 Vowels before final voiced consonants sound l-o-n-g-e-r than vowels before final voiceless consonants.

EXERCISE 5

A ◀) Listen. Repeat the word pairs. **CD 1; Track 33**

Voiceless	Voiced		Voiceless	Voiced
1. lap	lab		6. tack	tag
2. seat	seed		7. leaf	leave
3. coat	code		8. proof	prove
4. rack	rag		9. peace	peas
5. buck	bug		10. price	prize

B ◀) Listen again to the word pairs in part **A**. Repeat the words silently. Do you notice the difference? **CD 1; Track 33**

TIP ▼ Pronunciation Practice Strategies

Here are some suggestions to make your pronunciation practice more interesting and effective.

- **Speak with your eyes closed**; your ears will be more alert.
- **Speak silently**; this will draw your attention to the movement of your mouth and tongue.
- **Speak in slow motion**; this will also allow you to focus on the movement of your mouth.

EXERCISE 6 **A** 🔊 Listen to the speaker say sentence *a* or *b*. Check ✓ the matching response.
CD 1; Track 34

1. a. Did you lo<u>ck</u> it?   ____ No, I didn't have the key.

   b. Did you lo<u>g</u> it?   ✓ Yes, I wrote it down.

2. a. I heard about the ra<u>c</u>e.   ____ Who won?

   b. I heard about the rai<u>s</u>e.   ____ How much was it?

3. a. Did she make the be<u>t</u>?   ____ No, she didn't have the money.

   b. Did she make the be<u>d</u>?   ____ Yes, she's very neat.

4. a. Should I put it in the ba<u>ck</u>?   ____ No, in the front.

   b. Should I put it in the ba<u>g</u>?   ____ Yes, in the big blue one.

5. a. I forgot my lab coa<u>t</u>.   ____ You can wear mine.

   b. I forgot my lab co<u>de</u>.   ____ Ask for a new number.

6. a. Take a ca<u>p</u>.   ____ Is it sunny out?

   b. Take a ca<u>b</u>.   ____ No, I think I'll walk.

B 🔊 Check your answers with your class. Then listen and repeat the sentences and responses in part **A** with your eyes closed. CD 1; Track 35

C Work with a partner. Look again at the sentences in part **A**. Student A, say sentence *a* or *b*. Student B, say the matching response. Remember, vowels before voiced consonants are longer.

Did you lock it?   No, I didn't have the key.

A Read the situation. Follow the instructions.

Situation: You have just left class. Your teacher, who is still in the classroom, is waving a cell phone and trying to tell you something through the window.

Teacher: Say the message on page 31 without your voice. Just move your lips. Students: Write the message your teacher says in the bubble.	

B Work with a partner. Student A, look at this page. Student B, turn to page 31. Read the situations and say your messages without your voice. Write the messages your partner says in the bubbles.

1. Situation: Students are sitting in a classroom listening to a lecture. One student is asking another classmate a question.

Student B: Say the message. Student A: Write the message.	

2. Situation: Two friends are at a boring party. One friend asks the other a question.

Student B: Say the message. Student A: Write the message.	

3. Situation: A college student sees his roommate in a crowded, noisy hallway.

Student A: Say the message. Student B: Write the message.	Your dad will call you at five!

4. Situation: A husband and wife are attending a dinner party. One tells the other something.

Student A: Say the message. Student B: Write the message.	You have food in your teeth!

C Work in a small group. What did you notice about mouth movements when you were speaking silently? Tell your group. Have you ever been in a similar situation? Tell your group about the situation and the message.

A  Listen to the voicemail message about an astronomy club meeting. Read silently as you listen. Move your mouth as you read. CD 1; Track 36

Astronomy Club

"This is a message for J**en**. My name is W**ade**, and

I'm calling about the new astronomy club meeting.

We mee**t** Friday nigh**t** at eight o'clo**ck** in r**oo**m **five**

of T**eeg** Hall. We'll learn to **u**se our new telesco**pe**.

I'll email a meeting plan by n**oo**n tomorrow.

Pl**ea**se loo**k** at it before we mee**t**. See you s**oo**n!"

B Work with a partner. Take turns saying the message.

C Record yourself saying the message. Listen to your recording. Circle the words with underlined sounds that you said correctly. Re-record if necessary. When you are ready, submit your recording to your teacher.

A Teacher: Say the message without your voice. Just move your lips. Students will write the message.

> **Message:** You forgot your phone!

B Student B, look at this page. Student A, look at page 29. Read the situations and say your messages to your partner without your voice. Write the messages your partner says in the bubbles.

1. Situation: Students are sitting in a classroom listening to a lecture. One student is asking another classmate a question.

Student B: Say the message. Student A: Write the message.	Did you do your homework?

2. Situation: Two friends are at a boring party. One friend asks the other a question.

Student B: Say the message. Student A: Write the message.	Can we leave at eight?

3. Situation: A college student sees his roommate in a crowded, noisy hallway.

Student A: Say the message. Student B: Write the message.	

4. Situation: A husband and wife are attending a dinner party. One tells the other something.

Student A: Say the message. Student B: Write the message.	

C Work in a small group. What did you notice about mouth movements when you were speaking silently? Tell your group. Have you ever been in a similar situation? Tell your group about the situation and the message.

OBJECTIVES

In this chapter, you will learn:

- the importance of pronouncing *-s* endings clearly.
- the grammatical forms that take *-s* endings.
- the different pronunciations of the *-s* ending.

SUMMARY

The grammatical *-s* endings have three possible pronunciations. Luckily, there are guidelines to help you. This chapter will present the pronunciation guidelines. It will also provide the practice and strategies you need to say the endings correctly.

Warm Up

EXERCISE 1 **A** Work with a partner. Look at each business card. What does each person do? Write two sentences.

City Photo & Video	Cat Crazy Cat Sitting
• family photos • wedding & reception photo & video • digital or CD copies Maria Vassera, owner 800-555-8435 mvasseraphoto@mail.com	Don't worry while you're away. We'll: • feed your cats • play with them • clean up messes • give medicine Catherine Strayd, owner (202) 555-0152 www.catcrazy.net

1. Maria takes pictures at weddings.

   She also makes videos.

2. _____

Prayma Patel
*Assistant Professor
English*

400 Hill St., Room 1205
Morris, NJ 07963
patel@jcc.edu
973-555-3334

Jersey Community College

Digital Dan

• repair and service
• laptops, tablets, smart phones
• 9:00-9:00 every day
• 316-555-8221

digital_dan@fixit.net

3. _____   4. _____

_____   _____

_____   _____

_____   _____

B Dictate your answers to your teacher. With your class, identify all of the words that have -*s* at the end.

Notice

EXERCISE 2   **A** 🔊 Listen. The speaker will say sentence *a* or *b*. Circle the one you hear. **CD 1; Track 37**

1. a. Could you feed my <u>cat</u>?
   b. Could you feed my <u>cats</u>?

2. a. He left his business <u>card</u>.
   b. He left his business <u>cards</u>.

3. a. Ari works with his <u>cousin</u>.
   b. Ari works with his <u>cousins</u>.

4. a. When did your <u>guest</u> arrive?
   b. When did your <u>guests</u> arrive?

5. a. Let me wash the <u>dish</u>.
   b. Let me wash the <u>dishes</u>.

6. a. Who sent the <u>rose</u>?
   b. Who sent the <u>roses</u>?

7. a. Did you get my <u>message</u>?
   b. Did you get my <u>messages</u>?

8. a. Do you have to pay the <u>tax</u>?
   b. Do you have to pay the <u>taxes</u>?

B 🔊 Check your answers with your class. Then listen to both sentences in each pair from part **A**. Do you notice a difference? **CD 1; Track 38**

DID YOU KNOW? Omitting the final -*s* can create problems for listeners.

• Sometimes the meaning is not clear.
  John hit a tree and broke his leg(s).
• Sometimes the meaning is clear, but the missing -*s* distracts the listener.
  My teacher give(s) two quiz(zes) every Friday.

We use -s endings for these forms.

Simple present: Dr. Adams teaches at 10:00. He loves teaching. (3rd person, singular)

Plurals: Liz loves her cats. She doesn't have any dogs.

Possessives: Lee's bag is in Mike's car.

Contractions: He's going to China. He's traveled all over the world.

Final -s Sounds

🔊 We pronounce -s endings in three ways. Listen. Do you hear /s/, /z/, or /əz/?
Circle the sound you hear. **CD 1; Track 39**

Group 1: pets, sleeps, Mike's	/s/	/z/	/əz/
Group 2: dogs, drives, Lee's	/s/	/z/	/əz/
Group 3: faxes, teaches, Rose's	/s/	/z/	/əz/

RULE 5.1

Group 1: If the word ends in a voiceless sound (cat, sleep, Mike), add an /s/ sound.

Group 2: If the word ends in a voiced sound (dog, drive, Lee), add a /z/ sound.

Group 3: If the word ends in a hissing /s/ or a buzzing sound (fax, teach, Rose), add another syllable: /əz/ or /ɪz/.

**"I can't believe I went out with an apostrophe.
He was so possessive."**

EXERCISE 3   **A** 🔊 Listen and repeat the words in the chart. CD 1; Track 40

/s/	/z/	/əz/ or /ɪz/
likes	needs	dishes
tapes	songs	watches
coats	keys	closes
laughs	phones	messages
drinks	wears	practices
Pat's cats	Bob's jobs	Jess's dresses
		bosses

B Work with a partner. Take turns saying the words in the box. Then write each word in the correct column in part **A**.

~~bosses~~	desks	Jeff's	Liz's	meetings	taxes
copies	emails	laptops	Lou's	offices	works

C 🔊 Listen to the complete chart in part **A** and check your answers. Then listen again and say the words with the speaker. CD 1; Track 41

Sound and Spelling: -es

Don't let the -es spelling confuse you. Sometimes adding -s to a word with -e does not create a new syllable.

tap	→	**tap**		**tap**	→	**tap**
love		loves		hope		hopes
see		sees		date		dates

Sometimes it does add a syllable.

tap	→	**tap** – *tap*		**tap**	→	**tap** – *tap*
house /s/		hous - es		face /s/		fac - es
page /dʒ/		pag - es		size /z/		siz - es

RULE 5.2 Remember, the -es sounds like the syllable /əz/ or the word *is* /ɪz/ only after hissing or buzzing sounds: /s, z, ʃ, ʒ, tʃ, dʒ/.

📍 **CHOOSE YOUR PATH**

• For more practice with *hissing* sounds (ʃ, ʒ, tʃ, dʒ), turn to Consonant Sounds 14, page 166.

EXERCISE 4 🔊 Listen. Then repeat the words and sentences. As you say the words, tap a pen on your book. CD 1; Track 42

tap	→	*tap*	
1. love		loves	Lizzie <u>loves</u> animals.
2. write		writes	Naomi <u>writes</u> poetry.
3. name		names	Our teacher has finally learned our <u>names</u>.
4. wake		wakes	Marty <u>wakes</u> up at 7:00.

tap	→	*tap* – *tap*	
5. wash		wash - es	Amin <u>washes</u> his car on Sundays.
6. price		pric - es	Which store has the best <u>prices</u>?
7. bridge		bridg - es	Cross two <u>bridges</u> and then turn right.
8. box		box - es	We need two <u>boxes</u> of cereal.

EXERCISE 5 **A** Work with a partner. Student A, circle one of the words in the parentheses. Say the sentence with the word you circled. Student B, listen to Student A and check ✓ *Singular* or *Plural*.

	Singular	**Plural**
1. Which (suitcase, suitcases) did you take?	☐	☐
2. Do the (exercise, exercises) for homework.	☐	☐
3. Henry broke the (glass, glasses).	☐	☐
4. I visited the (beach, beaches).	☐	☐
5. Which (language, languages) did you study in school?	☐	☐
6. Pay the cashier for your (purchase, purchases).	☐	☐
7. Did you listen to your (message, messages)?	☐	☐
8. His (wish, wishes) came true.	☐	☐
9. The law (office is, offices are) around the corner.	☐	☐
10. The dirty (dish is, dishes are) in the sink.	☐	☐

B Check your answers with your partner. Then switch roles and repeat the activity.

📍 **CHOOSE YOUR PATH**

• For a *Word Search* puzzle to practice the pronunciation of -s endings, turn to Consonant Sounds 9, page 151.
• For practice with -s endings and linking, continue with the chapter.

TIP ▼ Linking -s Endings with the Next Word

For smoother, more natural speech, link the -s ending to the first sound in the next word.

- Link the -s ending to a vowel sound.
  Zia gets up at 5:00 in the morning. (sounds like *get-sup*)

- Link the -s ending to an /s/ sound.
  Javier feels sick. (sounds like *feel-sick*)

- Link the -s ending to another consonant sound.
  Omar likes noodles. (sounds like *like-snoodles*)

EXERCISE 6 **A** Draw a link from the word ending with -s to the first sound of the next word. Say the phrases silently as you link the words.

1. _____ often cooks at home.

2. _____ often sleeps until noon.

3. _____ often rides a bike to school.

4. _____ often loses stuff.

5. _____ often sings in the shower.

6. _____ never eats lunch.

7. _____ never drinks coffee.

8. _____ never gets sad.

9. _____ never misses class.

10. _____ never uses pencils.

B Look at the activities in part **A**. Walk around your classroom. Find someone who *often/never* does each activity. Find as many people as you can in five minutes. Write their names in the spaces.

| Do you often cook at home? | Yes, almost every day. |

| What's your name? | Sam. |

C Share one or two of your answers with the class.

Sam often cooks at home.

Communicative Practice Describe Your Dream Job

A Imagine your dream job. Draw your business card. Include the most useful information about your job. See pages 32–33 for ideas.

B Work with a partner. Describe your job and your job duties to your partner. Listen to your partner describe his or her job, and take notes here.

____

____

____

____

C Describe your partner's dream job to a small group or to the class. Tell what your partner does.

A 🔊 Listen. Fill in the blanks with the words you hear. CD 1; Track 43

Odd Jobs

1. John is an ice-cream taster (also called a food scientist). He _____tastes_____ ice cream and _____gets_____ paid to do it! The average yearly salary for this job is 56,000 dollars.

2. Cindy is a personal shopper. If someone _____ new clothing but doesn't have time to shop, she _____ clothes or even shoes for them. Personal _____ can make between 25,000 and 100,000 or more _____ per year!

3. Brian is a professional video gamer. He _____ video games for a living. The top paid video gamer _____ over 400,000 dollars a year. The annual salary of a professional gamer is from 85,000 to 400,000 dollars or more.

4. Jenny is a horse exerciser. She _____ racehorses. She loves _____ and riding, so this is a perfect job for her. _____ salary is around 50,000 dollars a year.

B Check your answers with the class. Then work with a partner. Choose your two favorite odd jobs and practice saying them with your partner.

C When you are ready, record yourself saying the job descriptions. Listen and check your -*s* endings. Re-record if necessary. Then submit your recording to your teacher.

CHAPTER **6** The *-ed* Ending

OBJECTIVES

In this chapter, you will learn:

- the importance of pronouncing *-ed* endings clearly.
- the grammatical forms that take *-ed* endings.
- the different pronunciations of the *-ed* ending.

SUMMARY

The grammatical ending *-ed* has three possible pronunciations. This chapter will present the pronunciation guidelines. It will also provide the practice and strategies you need to say the endings correctly.

Warm Up

EXERCISE 1   **A** 🔊 Julio has called to tell a friend about his first day of college. Complete his message with the words you hear. **CD 1; Track 44**

First Day on Campus

"It was terrible! First, I got lost and (1) _____arrived_____ about 20 minutes late to

my first class. The professor (2) _____ at me angrily. I sat down, very

nervous and upset. I (3) _____ and took notes for ten minutes before

I (4) _____ I was in the wrong class! I left quietly. I (5) _____

my first class completely but ran to my second class and (6) _____

a few times to be sure it was the correct room. It was, and that class was fine.

I even (7) _____ a few questions during the class. After class, I went

back to my dorm room and took a nap. I was (8) _____ !

B Check your answers with your class.

C 🔊 Listen again. Did you hear *-ed* endings on all of the verbs? **CD 1; Track 44**

EXERCISE 2   **A** 🔊 Listen. The speaker will say sentence *a* or *b*. Circle the one you hear.
CD 1; Track 45

1. (a.) My parents always <u>arrive</u> on time.

   b. My parents always <u>arrived</u> on time.

2. a. Shops <u>close</u> at 9:00 p.m. on Sundays.

   b. Shops <u>closed</u> at 9:00 p.m. on Sundays.

3. a. Janet and Sonia <u>want</u> a higher salary.

   b. Janet and Sonia <u>wanted</u> a higher salary.

4. a. I <u>like</u> watching cartoons.

   b. I <u>liked</u> watching cartoons.

5. a. We <u>need</u> to get better grades.

   b. We <u>needed</u> to get better grades.

6. a. My brothers <u>work</u> in the city.

   b. My brothers <u>worked</u> in the city.

B 🔊 Check your answers with your class. Then listen to both sentences in each pair in part **A**. Do you notice a difference between present and past? CD 1; Track 46

EXERCISE 3   **A** 🔊 Listen and write the number of syllables in each word. CD 1; Track 47

1. grade	_1_	6. open	_____
graded	_2_	opened	_____
2. play	_____	7. lock	_____
played	_____	locked	_____
3. call	_____	8. hope	_____
called	_____	hoped	_____
4. wait	_____	9. sound	_____
waited	_____	sounded	_____
5. visit	_____	10. miss	_____
visited	_____	missed	_____

B 🔊 Check your answers with your class. Then listen again. Do you notice that sometimes the *-ed* ending is a sound and sometimes it is a syllable?
CD 1; Track 47

Rules and Practice

We use the *-ed* ending for these forms.

Simple past: Javier watch**ed** a movie last night.

Past participles: Luz has want**ed** a cat for many years.

Participial adjectives: The audience was bor**ed**.

Final *-ed* Sounds

🔊 We pronounce final *-ed* three ways. Listen to *-ed* in each group. Do you hear /t/, /d/, or /əd/?

Circle the sound you hear. **CD 1; Track 48**

Group 1: need**ed**, rest**ed**, start**ed**   /t/   /d/   /əd/

Group 2: plann**ed**, mov**ed**, call**ed**   /t/   /d/   /əd/

Group 3: pick**ed**, miss**ed**, thank**ed**   /t/   /d/   /əd/

RULE 6.1

Group 1: If the word ends in a /t/ or /d/ (res**t**, nee**d**), add the syllable /əd/ or /ɪd/.

Group 2: If the word ends in a voiced sound (pla**n**, mo**ve**), add a /d/ sound.

Group 3: If the word ends in a voiceless sound (pi**ck**, mi**ss**), add a /t/ sound.

TIP ▼ The Difference Between a Voiceless and Voiced Sound

If you aren't sure whether a consonant sound is voiceless or voiced, put your hands over your ears and say the sound. You will hear and feel the vibration of the voiced sound. Notice the difference when you say these voiceless and voiced pairs.

/p, b/   /k, g/   /s, z/   /t, d/   /f, v/

EXERCISE 4 **A** 🔊 Listen and repeat the words in the chart. CD 1; Track 49

/əd/ or /ɪd/	/t/	/d/
added	asked	applied
exhausted	finished	caused
needed	passed	closed
waited	washed	opened
wanted	worked	used
acted		

B Work with a partner. Take turns saying the words in the box. Then write each word in the correct column in part **A**.

~~acted~~	decided	laughed	missed	planted	stopped
changed	graduated	looked	moved	stayed	tired

C 🔊 Listen to the complete chart in part **A** and check your answers. Then listen again and say the words with the speaker. CD 1; Track 50

DID YOU KNOW ?

The *-ed* sound usually links to the next word.
- When the word after *-ed* begins with a vowel, the past tense ending is clear.
  They lived in Cairo. (sounds like *live-din*)
- When the word after *-ed* begins with /d/ or /t/, the past tense ending is hard to hear.
  Javier looked tired. (sounds like *look-tired*)

EXERCISE 5 **A** Work with a partner. Student A, read sentence *a* (present) or *b* (past). Student B, say the sentence you hear—*a* or *b*. Then switch roles and repeat the activity.

1. a. We never <u>use</u> our gym membership.

   b. We never <u>used</u> our gym membership.

2. a. I <u>work</u> too many hours.

   b. I <u>worked</u> too many hours.

3. a. We <u>play</u> a lot of online games.

   b. We <u>played</u> a lot of online games.

4. a. We <u>cook</u> a lot.

   b. We <u>cooked</u> a lot.

5. a. I <u>laugh</u> at a lot of cat videos.

   b. I <u>laughed</u> at a lot of cat videos.

6. a. We <u>listen</u> to 90s music.

   b. We <u>listened</u> to 90s music.

7. a. I <u>study</u> every night.

   b. I <u>studied</u> every night.

8. a. She <u>sounds</u> upset.

   b. She <u>sounded</u> upset.

B Discuss your answers. Did you hear the sentences your partner said? Which two sentences had an *-ed* ending that was more difficult to hear?

C 🔊 Now listen to both sentences in each pair from part **A**. Say each sentence with the speaker. Remember to link the *-ed* ending to the next word. **CD 1; Track 51**

📍 **CHOOSE YOUR PATH**

• For a *Word Search* puzzle to practice the pronunciation of *-ed* endings, turn to Consonant Sounds 9, page 152.

• For communicative practice with *-ed* endings, continue with the chapter.

Communicative Practice   Life Stories

A Work with a partner. Practice saying the verb forms in the box.

applied	got divorced	graduated	visited	realized
finished	got hired	immigrated	moved from	returned
got accepted to	got married	learned	played	started

B Look at Maria's timeline. Take turns reading her timeline information to your partner.

In 2007, Maria arrived in the United States. From 2007 to...

Maria's Timeline

Arrived in the US	Studied English	Worked in a hospital	Graduated from nursing school
2007	2007–2008	2008–2009	2013

C On the timeline below, write four important events in your life (or the life of someone you admire). Write the years beneath the events.

_____ **Timeline**
(name)

years   _____   _____   _____   _____

D Share your timelines in small groups. Ask members of your group questions.

In 2010, I immigrated to the United States from Russia.

Did you come alone?

Yes, but my mother and brother arrived a year later.

A 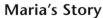 Listen to Maria's story. Write the words you hear to complete the story.
CD 1; Track 52

Maria's Story

I first came to the United States in 2007. I (1) _____studied_____ English

for a year. My plan was to go to college and study nursing. I

(2) _____ to work with children in Africa or South America.

After one year, I (3) _____ to several universities but wasn't

(4) _____ to any. I was very (5) _____ . I almost quit.

But I didn't. Instead, I (6) _____ for a year in a hospital and then

(7) _____ again. This time I was successful! Four years later, I

(8) _____ .

B Check your answers with your class. Then listen again and read silently with Maria. Pay attention to the final *-ed* sounds and the linking.

C Practice reading Maria's story with a partner. When you are ready, record yourself reading the story. Listen and check your pronunciation of the words with *-ed* endings. Re-record if necessary. Then submit your recording to your teacher.

PART III Word Stress

The staff of the West Lake Restaurant take a break in Changsha, China.

OBJECTIVES

In this chapter, you will learn:

- to make syllables in words sound stressed.
- to use simple guidelines to determine the stress in numbers, nouns, and verbs.

SUMMARY

In words with two or more syllables, one syllable is stronger than the others. This syllable is stressed. Listeners depend on stress patterns to identify the words they hear. So when you learn new words and phrases, it is important to learn the stress patterns, too.

The Sahara is a **de**sert.   I like ice cream for des**sert**.

Warm Up

EXERCISE 1   **A** 🔊 Listen. Circle the word you hear. Then check ✓ the correct response.
CD 1; Track 53

1. I was so busy today. First, I returned that book on Southwestern (**de**serts / (des**serts**)).

   ___ Oh, do you like geography?
   ✓ Oh, do you like to cook?

2. Yes, I do. Then I got that (**mes**sage / mas**sage**) I've been waiting for.

   ___ I hope it was good news.
   ___ That sounds relaxing!

3. It was. Then I spoke to Jen about the new (**com**edy / com**mit**tee).

   ___ Did she think it was funny?
   ___ Oh, is she a member, too?

4. Yes. Then I had to pick up pizza for a party of (**for**ty / four**teen**) kids!

   ___ Wow! That's over ten pizzas!
   ___ That's three or four pizzas!

B 🔊 Check your answers with your class. Then listen to the complete conversation.
CD 1; Track 54

Notice

EXERCISE 2 **A** 🔊 Listen. Check ✔ the word or phrase you hear. CD 1; Track 55

1. ___ thirty   ✔ thirteen

2. ___ tulips   ___ two lips

3. ___ message   ___ massage

4. ___ often   ___ offend

5. ___ element   ___ a limit

6. ___ common   ___ come on

7. ___ object (n)   ___ object (v)

8. ___ eleven   ___ elephant

B 🔊 Check your answers with your class. Then listen to both words in each pair. Do you notice a difference? CD 1; Track 56

DID YOU KNOW ? When word stress is wrong, your listener might not understand you, even if all your sounds are correct. For example, if you stress the wrong syllable, *des**sert*** might sound like ***de**sert*. If you stress all syllables in ***spe-cial-ty***, it might sound like ***special tea***.

EXERCISE 3 **A** 🔊 Listen for the stressed syllable. You will hear **DA**-də or də-**DA**. Circle the one you hear. CD 1; Track 57

1. (**DA**-də)   də-**DA**

2. **DA**-də   (də-**DA**)

3. **DA**-də   də-**DA**

4. **DA**-də   də-**DA**

5. **DA**-də   də-**DA**

6. **DA**-də   də-**DA**

B 🔊 Listen to the words. Which stress pattern do you hear, **DA**-də or də-**DA**? Circle the correct pattern. CD 1; Track 58

1. promise	(**DA**-də)	də-**DA**
2. result	**DA**-də	(də-**DA**)
3. succeed	**DA**-də	də-**DA**
4. famous	**DA**-də	də-**DA**
5. present (n.)	**DA**-də	də-**DA**
6. present (v.)	**DA**-də	də-**DA**
7. record (n.)	**DA**-də	də-**DA**
8. record (v.)	**DA**-də	də-**DA**
9. enjoy	**DA**-də	də-**DA**
10. method	**DA**-də	də-**DA**
11. fifteen	**DA**-də	də-**DA**
12. sister	**DA**-də	də-**DA**

Rules and Practice

Stress in Numbers

🔊 Listen to the stress patterns in these numbers. CD 1; Track 59

ₒ ◯	◯ ₒ
four**teen**	**for**ty
six**teen**	**six**ty
eigh**teen**	**eigh**ty

RULE 7.1 The -*teen* numbers are usually stressed on the -*teen* syllable. The ten numbers are usually stressed on the first syllable.

TIP ▼ *Thirty* or *Thirteen*?

When you listen to North American English, another way to distinguish between numbers like *thirty* and *thirteen* is the pronunciation of /t/. In -*teen* numbers, /t/ is clearly pronounced. However, in most ten numbers like *thirty*, /t/ sounds like a quick /d/: *thirdy, sevendy, eighdy*.

EXERCISE 4 **A** 🔊 Listen to the speaker say sentence *a* or *b*. Check ✔ the sentence you hear. CD 1; Track 60

1. a. Class begins at 4:15.
   b. Class begins at 4:50.   ✔

2. a. I'd like to make a reservation for 18.   ___
   b. I'd like to make a reservation for 80.   ___

3. a. That'll be $4.16.   ___
   b. That'll be $4.60.   ___

4. a. I live at eight ninety (890) Green Street.   ___
   b. I live at eight nineteen (819) Green Street.   ___

5. a. Our party's on the thirteenth.   ___
   b. Our party's on the thirtieth.   ___

6. a. The movie starts at 7:15.   ___
   b. The movie starts at 7:50.   ___

7. a. Your flight to Seoul leaves from Gate 14.   ___
   b. Your flight to Seoul leaves from Gate 40.   ___

8. a. She's 17.   ___
   b. She's 70.   ___

9. a. The room is 12 by 13.   ___
   b. The room is 12 by 30.   ___

10. a. Take bus number 19.   ___
    b. Take bus number 90.   ___

B 🔊 Check your answers with your class. Then listen to both sentences in each pair from part **A**. Repeat each sentence. CD 1; Track 61

C Work with a partner. Student A, look at part **A**, numbers 1–5. Circle *a* or *b* and say it to your partner. Student B, circle the letter your partner said. Then switch roles for numbers 6–10. Check your answers.

Stress in Two-Syllable Nouns

🔊 Listen to these two-syllable nouns. Notice the stress pattern. CD 1; Track 62

◯　◦

country

doctor

tablet

RULE 7.2 Stress the first syllable of most two-syllable nouns. About 90 percent of all two-syllable nouns have first-syllable stress.

Stress in Two-Syllable Verbs

🔊 Listen to these two-syllable verbs. Notice the stress pattern. CD 1; Track 63

◦　◯

en**joy**

dis**cuss**

sub**tract**

RULE 7.3 Stress the second syllable of most two-syllable verbs. About 60 percent of all two-syllable verbs have second-syllable stress.

EXERCISE 5 **A** 🔊 Listen and repeat the words in the chart. CD 1; Track 64

Two-Syllable Nouns	Two-Syllable Verbs
apple	a**gree**
problem	be**have**
student	oc**cur**
teacher	pro**tect**
_____	advise
_____	_____
_____	_____
_____	_____

B Work with a partner. Take turns saying the words in the box. Then write each word in the correct column in part **A**.

advise	college	decide	mother
believe	complain	essay	reason

C 🔊 Listen to the complete chart in part **A** and check your answers. Then listen again and say the words with the speaker. CD 1; Track 65

D Work with a partner. Think of five more two-syllable nouns and two-syllable verbs and write them in the chart. Say the words. Do your words follow the rules? Remember, you will find exceptions.

Two-Syllable Nouns	Two-Syllable Verbs
1. _____	1. _____
2. _____	2. _____
3. _____	3. _____
4. _____	4. _____
5. _____	5. _____

TIP ▼ **Use Your Dictionary**

Remember, you can use your dictionary to check for stress. Most dictionaries use a ' symbol before the stressed syllable.

ta•ble /'te^y bəl/   re-act /ri^y 'ækt /

Stress in Two-Syllable Noun and Verb Pairs

🔊 Sometimes the same word is used as a noun and a verb. Listen to these noun–verb pairs. Notice the stress patterns. CD 1; Track 66

Nouns	Verbs
◯ ∘ **pro**duce	∘ ◯ pro**duce**
record	re**cord**

RULE 7.4 When the same two-syllable word is used as both a noun and a verb, we usually stress the first syllable when the word is a noun. We stress the second syllable when the word is a verb.

EXERCISE 6 **A** Work with a partner. Student A, say either the noun or verb form from the chart. Student B, say the other form.

con**duct** ▶ **con**duct

Academic		Business		Law	
Noun	Verb	Noun	Verb	Noun	Verb
conduct	con**duct**	**con**tract	con**tract**	**con**vict	con**vict**
project	pro**ject**	**in**crease	in**crease**	**ob**ject	ob**ject**
progress	pro**gress**	**pro**duce	pro**duce**	**per**mit	per**mit**
present	pre**sent**	**re**call	re**call**	**sus**pect	sus**pect**

Note: Not *all* two-syllable noun–verb pairs change stress; for example: an **an**swer / to **an**swer; a de**lay** / to de**lay**; a re**port** / to re**port**; a **pro**mise / to **pro**mise; a re**ply** / to re**ply**.

B Switch roles with your partner and repeat part **A**.

EXERCISE 7 **A** Work with a partner. Circle the correct word.

1. The (**pro**duce / pro**duce**) is in the back, past the milk and eggs.

2. What companies (**pro**duce / pro**duce**) cars in the U.S.?

3. He signed the (**con**tract / con**tract**), but he could not do the work.

4. Can you (**con**duct / con**duct**) a web meeting easily?

5. Is the (**de**crease / de**crease**) in book sales because of the rise in e-books?

6. The camera didn't work. The store gave me a full (**re**fund / re**fund**).

7. Click here to (**re**cord / re**cord**) yourself. Press the arrow to hear your recording.

8. My phone battery dies after one hour! It's time for an (**up**grade / up**grade**).

9. The city does not (**per**mit / per**mit**) fishing on public beaches.

10. A large (**pro**test / pro**test**) is planned in front of the state building this Friday.

11. Have you made any (**pro**gress / pro**gress**) on your research paper?

12. Does anyone (**ob**ject / ob**ject**) to these dates for the conference?

13. Our (**pro**ject / pro**ject**) is finally complete. Let's celebrate!

14. She will (**pre**sent / pre**sent**) the new product ideas at the next meeting.

B 🔊 Listen and check your answers. Then practice saying the sentences in part **A** with a partner. CD 1; Track 67

Stress in Compound Nouns

🔊 Listen to these compound nouns. Notice the stress. **CD 1; Track 68**

○   ○

classroom

mailbox

flashlight

RULE 7.5 The stress is on the first word or first part of the compound noun.

Note: Sometimes the compound noun is written as two words: **cell** phone, **health** center. It is still pronounced as one word, with the first word receiving primary stress.

EXERCISE 8   **A** 🔊 Listen to these compound nouns. Then listen again and say them with the speaker. As you say the stressed syllable, tap your pen or your hand on your desk. **CD 1; Track 69**

baseball	**dead**line	**lap**top	**rest**room
bedroom	**head**phones	**note**book	**tool**bar
birthday	**help** desk	**pass**port	**voice**mail
bookstore	**home**work	**pass**word	**web**site

B Work with a partner. Think of five more compound nouns.

1. _____

2. _____

3. _____

4. _____

5. _____

C Share your words with your class. Put any new words in your *Personal Key Word List* in Appendix A on page A1.

A Student A, look at this page. Student B, look at page 58. Mark the syllable stress on the underlined words in blue. Use large and small dots. Check your stress marks with your class.

Troubles with Technology

A: Argh! This computer is so slow! I want to get this new (1) <u>software</u>, but it says I don't have enough (2) <u>disk space</u>.

B: I'm afraid it's time for you to (3) ____invest____ in a new (4) _____ .

A: It seems like I have to buy a new (5) <u>laptop</u> and (6) <u>cell phone</u> every year!

B: I know. I (7) _____ the companies make a lot of money on all these (8) _____ .

A: That's for sure. And they (9) <u>release</u> so many new (10) <u>products</u> every year. It (11) <u>creates</u> so much (12) <u>garbage</u>.

B: That's true. That can't be good for the (13) _____ . You can sell your old (14) _____ online, you know. I'll send you the link to one (15) _____ I know.

A: Great. Thanks. Now let's try to make some (16) <u>progress</u> on this project.

B Work with Student B. Take turns saying your lines. Write the missing words that your partner says in the spaces in part **A**.

C 🔊 Check your answers with your partner. Then listen to the conversation. CD 1; Track 70

D Practice the conversation with your partner.

A Read the announcement. With a partner, mark the syllable stress on the underlined words. Use large and small dots.

Workshop: Creating a Successful Small Business

This <u>weekend</u>, my <u>college</u> will conduct a <u>workshop</u> for people who want to <u>create</u> or <u>expand</u> a business. The <u>leaders</u> all have over <u>forty</u> years of experience in small business. They will talk about how to:

- <u>define</u> a <u>concept</u>

- <u>achieve</u> a plan

- use <u>spreadsheets</u>

- <u>reduce</u> taxes

- <u>respond</u> to change

The first <u>session</u> <u>begins</u> at 8:30 a.m. <u>Breakfast</u> and lunch will be served.

B Check your stress marks in part **A** with your class. Then listen to the announcement. CD 1; Track 71

C Work with a partner. Take turns saying the announcement. Monitor your partner's stress in the underlined words.

D When you are ready, record the announcement. Listen and check your stress in the underlined words. Re-record if necessary. Then submit your recording to your teacher.

Communicative Practice Troubles with Technology

A Student B, look at this page. Student A, look at page 56. Mark the syllable stress on the underlined words in blue. Use large and small dots. Check your stress marks with your teacher.

Troubles with Technology

A: Argh! This computer is so slow! I want to get this new (1) ___software___,

but it says I don't have enough (2) _____ .

B: I'm afraid it's time for you to (3) invest in a new (4) laptop.

A: It seems like I have to buy a new (5) _____ and (6) _____

every year!

B: I know. I (7) suspect the companies make a lot of money on all these

(8) products.

A: That's for sure. And they (9) _____ so many new

(10) _____ every year. It (11) _____ so much

(12) _____ .

B: That's true. That can't be good for the (13) planet. You can sell your old

(14) products online. I'll send you the link to one (15) website I know.

A: Great. Thanks. Now let's try to make some (16) _____ on this

project.

B Work with Student A. Take turns saying your lines. Write the missing words that your partner says in the spaces in part **A**.

C 🔊 Check your answers with your partner. Then listen to the conversation.
CD 1; Track 70

D Practice the conversation with your partner. Switch roles and practice again. Monitor your partner's stress in the underlined words.

CHAPTER 8 Stress in Words with Suffixes

OBJECTIVES

In this chapter, you will learn:

* to make syllables in words sound stressed.
* to predict stressed syllables in words with common suffixes.

SUMMARY

Suffixes are endings added to words. Some suffixes, such as *-ness,* do not change the stress of basic words (**hap**-py, **hap**-pi-*ness*). Other suffixes, such as *-ity,* do affect word stress (**a**-ble, a-**bi**-li-*ty*). This chapter provides general guidelines for suffixes that change word stress.

Warm Up

EXERCISE 1 **A** The way you sleep can tell something about your personality, according to some studies. Look at the sleep positions. Which position(s) do you usually sleep in? Check ✓ your most common position(s).

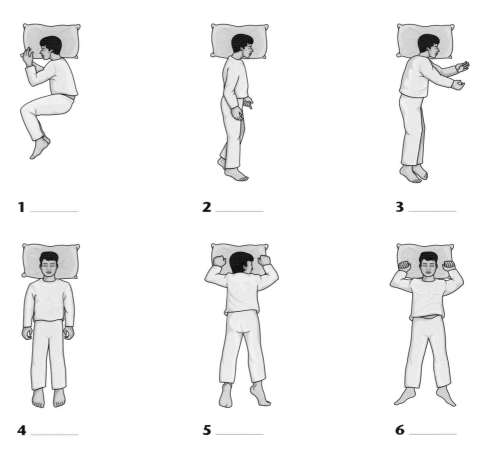

1 _____ 2 _____ 3 _____

4 _____ 5 _____ 6 _____

B Read the description(s) for your sleep position(s) from part **A**.

Sleep Position and Personality

1 At first, you appear strong and tough, but this may be a <u>protection</u> against the world. Your family and close friends see your <u>sensitivity</u>. The <u>majority</u> of people sleep in this <u>position</u>.

2 You love <u>conversation</u> and are known for your friendliness. Some people call you a "social butterfly." <u>Popularity</u> is important to you. This is the second most common sleep <u>position</u>, and health experts say it is good for your back.

3 You are known for your openness and <u>sincerity</u>. You like to try new things, but you can be suspicious of people or <u>situations</u>. You are often slow to make <u>decisions</u>. Experts say breathing is easier when you sleep on your side.

4 You are quiet, calm, and private. You seek <u>perfection</u> and have high <u>expectations</u> for yourself and others. This <u>position</u> may increase snoring, which can decrease your <u>ability</u> to breathe.

5 You appear confident and <u>energetic</u>. Some call you "the life of a party." At times, you appear nervous. You may become upset when people are <u>critical</u> of you. Experts say that lying on your stomach is good for your <u>digestion</u>.

6 You are a good friend and listener. You are known for your <u>generosity</u>. You do not like to be the center of <u>attention</u>. This <u>position</u> may increase snoring, which can decrease your <u>ability</u> to breathe.

C Write the underlined words from your description(s). Circle the syllable in each word that you think has primary stress. Share your words with a partner.

_____

_____

D Work in a group. Does your sleep position describe you? Tell your group why or why not.

> My position is number 5. The description says, "you appear confident and <u>energetic</u>." I think this is true.

Notice

EXERCISE 2   **A** 🔊 Listen. Circle the strongest syllable in each word. **CD 1; Track 72**

1. at-(tend)   at-(ten)-tion   6. per-so-nal   per-so-na-li-ty
2. de-cide   de-ci-sion   7. fan-ta-sy   fan-tas-tic
3. per-fect   per-fec-tion   8. e-ner-gy   e-ner-ge-tic
4. a-ble   a-bi-li-ty   9. mu-sic   mu-si-cian
5. po-pu-lar   po-pu-la-ri-ty   10. Ca-na-da   Ca-na-di-an

B 🔊 Check your answers with your class. Then listen again to both words in each pair. Do you notice what happens to the stress when the word forms change? **CD 1; Track 72**

Rules and Practice

🔊 These common suffixes do not change word stress: *-ness, -ful, -ment, -er.* Listen. **CD 1; Track 73**

happy	**hap**piness
beauty	**beau**tiful
re**quire**	re**quire**ment
em**ploy**	em**ploy**er

The following rules present the most common suffixes that *do* affect word stress.

Word Stress: Suffixes *-ion* and *-ity*

🔊 The suffixes *-ion* and *-ity* indicate a noun form. Listen. Where is the stress? **CD 1; Track 74**

-ion: ap**ply**   appli**ca**tion
-ity: **ma**jor   ma**jo**rity

RULE 8.1 The primary stress is on the syllable *before* the suffixes *-ion* and *-ity*.

EXERCISE 3   **A** 🔊 Listen. Say the words with the speaker. Open your fist on the stressed syllable.
CD 1; Track 75

va - **ca** - tion

va**ca**tion   a**bi**lity

de**ci**sion   elec**tri**city

per**fec**tion   perso**na**lity

edu**ca**tion   popu**la**rity

_____   capability

_____   _____

_____   _____

_____   _____

B Work with a partner. Add the suffix *-ion* or *-ity* to complete the words in the box.
Then write each word in the correct column in part **A**.

| capabil<u>ity</u> | informat_____ | permiss_____ | tuit_____ |
| graduat_____ | opportun_____ | possibil_____ | univers_____ |

C 🔊 Circle the stressed syllable in each word you wrote in part **A**. Then listen to
the complete chart and check your answers. CD 1; Track 76

D Work with a partner. Take turns saying the words in Part **A**. Open your fist
on the stressed syllables.

Word Stress: Suffixes *-ic* and *-ical*

🔊 The suffixes *-ic* and *-ical* indicate an adjective form. Listen. Where is the stress?
CD 1; Track 77

-ic: **ar**tist   ar**tis**tic

-ical: e**co**nomy   econo**mi**cal

RULE 8.2 The primary stress is on the syllable *before* the suffixes *-ic* and *-ical*.

EXERCISE 4   **A** 🔊 Complete the word in each sentence with *-ic* or *-ical*. Then listen and circle the stressed syllable in each *-ic/-ical* word. CD 1; Track 78

1. My brother is a me(cha)n<u>ic</u>. He fixes cars.

2. Jun eats only organ____ food. He thinks it's healthier.

3. I love cats, but I am allerg____ to them. They make me sneeze!

4. The firefighter was so brave. His actions were hero____.

5. This car is not very econom____. It uses a lot of gasoline.

6. Tula didn't sleep well last night, so she doesn't feel very energet____ today.

7. Martin exercises a lot. He's always been very athlet____.

8. I like to watch romant____ comedies.

9. That candidate doesn't belong to any polit____ party. She's independent.

10. You have to complete the application. It's crit____.

B 🔊 Listen again and check your answers. Say the sentences with the speaker. CD 1; Track 78

Word Stress: Suffix *-ian*

🔊 The suffix *-ian* indicates a noun, often a person. Listen. Where is the stress? CD 1; Track 79

-ian:	**li**brary	li**bra**rian
	Canada	Ca**na**dian
	comedy	co**me**dian

RULE 8.3 The primary stress is on the syllable *before* the suffix *-ian.*

Note: 1) Sometimes *-ian* is pronounced as two syllables, like the words in the chart. Sometimes *-ian* is pronounced as one syllable (e.g., e lec tri cian, po li ti cian). Check your dictionary to be sure. 2) See Appendix B for a more complete list of suffixes that affect word stress.

EXERCISE 5   **A** Work with a partner. Complete each sentence with a word that ends with *-ian*.
Circle the stressed syllable.

1. Someone who eats mostly vegetables is a ___vege(ta)rian___ .

2. Someone who works in a library is a _____ .

3. Someone who works in politics is a _____ .

4. Someone who studies history is a _____ .

5. Someone who fixes electrical problems is an _____ .

6. Someone born in Italy usually speaks _____ .

7. Someone who plays music is a _____ .

8. Someone who is from Canada is a _____ .

9. Someone who acts in a comedy is a _____ .

10. Someone who does magic is a _____ .

B Take turns reading the sentence starters in part **A**. Your partner will finish
the sentence with the correct *-ian* word.

Someone who eats mostly
vegetables is a. . .   vege**ta**rian.

TIP ▼ Unstressed Syllables

Remember, vowels in unstressed syllables are shorter and are often reduced to a schwa /ə/.
A schwa helps reduce the strength of unstressed syllables so that stressed syllables will be
more obvious.

It**a**lian   /ə' tæl yən/

de**ci**sion   /də 'sɪ ʒən/

EXERCISE 6   **A** Complete the words with the correct spelling of the schwa /ə/ sound.

1. _I_ **tal**ian   4. ec__**no**mic

2. __**pi**nion   5. **tel**__vision

3. defi**ni**t__n   6. mu**sic**__n

B 🔊 Listen and repeat the words. **CD 1; Track 80**

Communicative Activity | Qualities of a Successful Employee

A Work with a partner. Read the qualities of successful employees. Circle the stressed syllables in the underlined words. Then take turns saying the words.

<u>ability</u> to make <u>decisions</u>	<u>curiosity</u>	friendly <u>personality</u>
<u>ability</u> to solve problems	effective <u>communication</u> skills	good <u>education</u>
<u>attention</u> to detail	<u>energetic</u> manner	<u>reliability</u>
<u>creativity</u>	<u>flexibility</u>	<u>technical</u> knowledge

B With your partner, choose the three qualities from Part **A** that are most important for each of these occupations. Write them in the chart.

ESL Teacher	Electrician	Musician	Veterinarian

C Share your answers with your class. Give reasons for your choices.

An ESL teacher should have curi**o**sity about language and about other cultures. This helps students learn about the teacher and each other.

TIP ▼ Self-Monitoring

One way to improve your pronunciation is to self-monitor. Self-monitoring is listening to yourself and evaluating your pronunciation.

1. Record something you want to say.

2. Listen to your pronunciation of one or two features.

3. If you hear sounds or patterns that you want to improve, re-record and listen again.

A 🔊 Circle the stressed syllables in the underlined words of your most common sleep position(s). Then listen and read quietly with the speaker. **CD 1; Track 81**

Sleep Position and Personality

1 At first, you appear strong and tough, but this may be a <u>protection</u> against the world. Your family and close friends see your <u>sensitivity</u>. The <u>majority</u> of people sleep in this <u>position</u>.

2 You love <u>conversation</u> and are known for your friendliness. Some people call you a "social butterfly." <u>Popularity</u> is important to you. This is the second most common sleep <u>position</u>, and health experts say it is good for your back.

3 You are known for your openness and <u>sincerity</u>. You like to try new things, but you can be suspicious of people or <u>situations</u>. You are often slow to make <u>decisions</u>. Experts say breathing is easier when you sleep on your side.

4 You are quiet, calm, and private. You seek <u>perfection</u> and have high <u>expectations</u> for yourself and others. This <u>position</u> may increase snoring, which can decrease your <u>ability</u> to breathe.

5 You appear confident and <u>energetic</u>. Some call you "the life of a party." At times, you appear nervous. You may become upset when people are <u>critical</u> of you. Experts say that lying on your stomach is good for your <u>digestion</u>.

6 You are a good friend and listener. You are known for your <u>generosity</u>. You do not like to be the center of <u>attention</u>. This <u>position</u> may increase snoring, which can decrease your <u>ability</u> to breathe.

B Check your answers with your class. Then take turns reading your sleep position(s) aloud with a partner. Monitor your partner's stress patterns in the underlined words.

C When you are ready, record yourself reading your sleep position(s). Monitor your recording. Check your pronunciation of the underlined words. Re-record if necessary. Then submit your recording to your teacher.

PART IV Sentences: Rhythm and Connected Speech

Bikers resting after a ride in front of the Marina Bay, Singapore

9 Rhythm: Stressed Words

OBJECTIVES

In this chapter, you will learn:

- about English rhythm in phrases and sentences.
- which words are stressed.
- why words are stressed.

SUMMARY

Words have strong and weak beats:

com - **pu** - ter

So do sentences:

We **knew** her.

Strong beats receive stress. Weak beats do not. Like music or poetry, the pattern of strong and weak beats gives English its rhythm.

Warm Up

EXERCISE 1

A Your school made this announcement about a weather emergency. You must text the information to others quickly. Cross out any unnecessary words. Then rewrite the message as a text message.

Announcement	Text Message
"Classes are canceled on Tuesday due to the heavy snow. Updates will be on our website."	

B Work with a partner. Look at your text message from part **A**. Which words did you remove? Write them. _____

C Now look at your answers in part **B**. What kind of words did you remove? What kind of words did you keep? Tell your partner.

D 🔊 Listen to the full message from part **A**. What kind of words sound stronger in the message? What kind of words sound weaker? Discuss your answers with your class. CD 2; Track 2

EXERCISE 2   **A** 🔊 The following conversation is missing half of its words. Listen. Can you guess what the conversation is about? **CD 2; Track 3**

A: _____ was your _____ in _____?

B: I _____ a _____. _____ about _____?

A: A _____! I'm in _____. I _____ a _____ to _____
   to _____.

B: You'll be _____! You can _____ _____ in the _____.

B 🔊 Listen to the other half of the conversation. Now can you guess what it's about? **CD 2; Track 4**

A: What _____ _____ grade _____ math?

B: _____ think _____ B. How _____ yours?

A: _____ D! _____ _____ trouble. _____ need
   _____ C _____ apply _____ college.

B: _____ _____ fine! _____ _____ retake math
   _____ _____ summer.

C 🔊 Listen to the whole conversation. Notice the rhythm of the sentences.
CD 2; Track 5

> A: What was your grade in math?
>
> B: I think a B. How about yours?
>
> A: A D! I'm in trouble. I need a C to apply to college.
>
> B: You'll be fine! You can retake math in the summer.

D With your class, discuss these questions about the conversation.

1. What kinds of words are stressed and highlighted?

2. What kinds of words are unstressed and shaded?

Rules and Practice

Content Words and Sentence Stress

Content words give information in a sentence.

Content Words

Nouns	Main Verbs	Adjectives	Adverbs	Interjections	Wh- Words	Negative Auxiliaries
grade	think	fine	really	Wow!	what	can't
quiz	apply	happy	very	Yikes!	who	isn't
college	retake	bad	quickly	Aha!	when	don't

RULE 9.1 Content words are usually stressed. (**Yikes**! My **grade** on the **quiz** was **really bad**!)

Structure Words and Sentence Stress

Structure words are usually short words that make the grammar correct.

Structure Words

Articles	Prepositions	Pronouns	Auxiliaries	Conjunctions
a/an, the	in, at, with	he, she, it, they	can, do, is	but, so, and

RULE 9.2 Structure words are usually not stressed. (*Can you **help** me with my **math**?*)

TIP ▼ Stressing Content Words

When a content word has more than two syllables, stress only the stressed syllable.

*That **child** is **ve**ry cre**a**tive.*

EXERCISE 3 **A** Circle the content words.

1. It's (closed) on (Mondays).

2. Do you want me to call you?

3. Did you complete the application?

4. Tom and Lisa are absent.

5. Can we meet on Friday?

6. I'm not happy with my new laptop.

B 🔊 Check your answers with your class. Then listen and repeat the sentences. Remember to stress the content words or the stressed syllables of the content words. **CD 2; Track 6**

"**Sor**ry, I'm **late**, but I **did**n't **get** here on time."

EXERCISE 4 **A** 🔊 Listen and repeat these expressions commonly used by students.
CD 2; Track 7

1. **What's** the **an**swer to **num**ber **two**?

2. I'm **sor**ry. I **can't come** to **class** on **Mon**day.

3. Can I **bor**row a **piece** of **pa**per?

4. Could I **share** your **book**?

5. **Whose turn** is it?

6. Would you **mind check**ing my **home**work?

7. I was **late** because I **missed** the **bus**.

8. **What's** the **past tense** of "**write**"?

9. Could you ex**plain** the as**sign**ment?

10. I **missed** the **test** because I was **sick**.

B Work with a partner. Take turns saying the expressions in part **A**.

C With your partner, write two expressions that teachers often say in class. Circle the stressed words or syllables. Share your expressions with your class.

1. _____

2. _____

EXERCISE 5   **A**  Listen to the rhythm of this popular children's rhyme. Then listen again and say the rhyme with the speaker. **CD 2; Track 8**

◯ ◦ ◯ ◦
Humpty **Dump**ty

◯ ◦ ◦ ◯
sat on a **wall**.

◯ ◦ ◯ ◦
Humpty **Dump**ty

◯ ◦ ◦ ◯
had a great **fall**.

Note: In spoken English, *had a great fall* could have three stresses: ***had*** *a* ***great fall***.

B These common phrases and sentences have the same rhythm as "Humpty Dumpty." Listen and say the phrases and sentences after the speaker. **CD 2; Track 9**

◯ ◦ ◯ ◦ **Hump**ty **Dump**ty	◯ ◦ ◦ ◯ **Sat** on a **wall**
Nice to meet you.	What do you do?
What's the matter?	Where are you from?
How's it going?	What do you want?
Just a minute.	Give me a break.
Call your mother.	What is your name?

DID YOU KNOW ? Language is like music and poetry. It has rhythm. Every language has its own rhythm. English has strong beats and weak beats, but some languages have more equal beats. If you speak English with equal stress on all words or syllables, you could sound angry or rude.

◯ ◦ ◦ ◯ ◦
What are you **do**ing?   NOT

◯ ◯ ◯ ◯ ◯
What are you doing?

Be sure to *stress* content words and *weaken* structure words.

EXERCISE 6 **A** 🔊 Listen and say the sentences with the speaker. All of the sentences have the same three strong beats. Tap your pen in time to the beats. CD 2; Track 10

	tap	tap	tap
1.	↓	↓	↓
	Mice	**eat**	**cheese**.
The **mice** will	**eat**	the	**cheese**.
The **mice** will be	**eat**ing the		**cheese**.
The **mice** have been	**eat**ing the		**cheese**cake.

	tap	tap	tap
2.	↓	↓	↓
	Teachers	**give**	**tests**.
My **teach**ers	**give**	the	**tests**.
My **teach**ers will	**give**	us the	**tests**.
My **teach**ers are	**giv**ing	us the	**tests**.
My **teach**ers will be	**giv**ing us the		**tests**.

B Say the sentences in part **A** again with your class. Keep the beat by tapping your pen on your desk.

EXERCISE 7 **A** With a partner, complete these common expressions with a word or phrase from the box.

a ~~bee~~	a **fea**ther	**hon**ey	a **mouse**	a **pan**cake
a **bird**	a **ghost**	**ice**	an **owl**	**silk**

1. He's as **bu**sy as _____ a bee _____ .

2. She's as **white** as _____ .

3. You're as **sweet** as _____ .

4. She's as **wise** as _____ .

5. He **eats** like _____ .

6. He's as **qui**et as _____ .

7. It's as **flat** as _____ .

8. It's as **light** as _____ .

9. It's as **smooth** as _____ .

10. You're as **cold** as _____ .

B 🔊 Listen and check your answers. Then listen again and say the expressions with the speaker. Notice the rhythm of stressed and unstressed syllables. CD 2; Track 11

C Work with a partner. Take turns using the expressions from part **A** in new sentences. Monitor your partner's rhythm of stressed and unstressed syllables.

The **tea**cher's as **bu**sy as a **bee**.

Work with a partner. You will leave phone messages for each other. Student A, look at this page. Student B, turn to page 76.

A Student A, say your message to Student B.

> ### Student A's Message
>
> **Hi!** Do you **still want** to **go** on a **hike** this **Sa**turday? We should **leave** **ear**ly, at **se**ven or **eight**. **Call** me so we can **make** a **plan**. **Talk** to you **soon**.

B Listen to Student B's reply to your message. Write the missing words. Ask Student B to repeat the message if necessary.

> ### Student B's Reply
>
> _____. I _____ _____ on the _____.
>
> I _____ to _____. But I'm _____ on _____.
>
> _____ me if you'd _____ to _____ to a _____.

C 🔊 Check your answers with your partner. Then listen to the complete message and the reply. **CD 2; Track 12**

D With your partner, practice saying the message and the reply two more times. Use good rhythm.

A 🔊 A limerick is a type of funny or silly poem. It's usually five lines, with the first, second, and last line rhyming. Listen to these limericks. Notice the stressed words. **CD 2; Track 13**

Limericks

A **cir**cus per**for**mer named **Bri**an

Once **smiled** as he **rode** on a **li**on.

They came **back** from the **ride**,

But with **Bri**an in**side**,

And the **smile** on the **face** of the **li**on.

Anonymous

There **was** an old **man** of Pe**ru**

Who **dreamt** he was **eat**ing his **shoe**.

He **woke** in the **night**,

With a **ter**rible **fright**,

And **found** it was **per**fectly **true**.

Anonymous

There **was** a young **lad**y from **Leeds**

Who **swal**lowed a **pack**age of **seeds**.

Now this **sor**ry young **lass**

Is quite **cov**ered in **grass**,

But has **all** the to**ma**toes she **needs**.

Anonymous

B 🔊 Listen again. Say the limericks with the speaker. Try to keep the same rhythm. **CD 2; Track 13**

C Work with a partner. Take turns saying the limericks.

D Record yourself saying the limericks. Do the stressed words sound longer and clearer than the unstressed words? Re-record if necessary. Then submit your recording to your teacher.

A You are Student B. Listen to Student A's message. Write the missing words. Ask Student A to repeat the message if necessary.

Student A's Message

_____! Do you _____ _____ to _____ on a

_____ this _____?

We should _____ _____, at _____ or _____.

_____ me so we can _____ a _____. _____ to

you _____.

B Student B, say your reply to Student A.

Student B's Reply

Sorry. I **can't go** on the **hike**. I **have** to **work**. But I'm **free** on **Sun**day.

Call me if you'd **like** to **go** to a **mo**vie.

C 🔊 Check your answers with your partner. Then listen to the complete message and the reply. **CD 2; Track 12**

D With your partner, practice saying the message and the reply two more times. Use good rhythm.

CHAPTER **10** Rhythm: Reduced Words

OBJECTIVES

In this chapter, you will learn:

- that structure words are usually reduced.
- what reduced words sound like.
- how reduced words are weakened.

SUMMARY

Words such as *the, it,* and *of* are called *structure words*. In spoken English, structure words are usually weakened, or reduced, so that the more important content words are easier to hear.

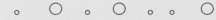

You've **shut** the **door** on my **hand**!

Warm Up

EXERCISE 1   **A** 🔊 Listen. Tom is on the phone. You hear only his half of the conversation. Circle the words you hear. **CD 2; Track 14**

... Yes. Mika's party is on Sunday at her house.

... That's right. It's (427)/ 4 to 7).

... I (can / can't) take you.

... Yeah. We're having cake and ice cream.

... I'll ask (for / four) volunteers to help.

... Victor (can / can't) come, but he (can / can't) buy the gift.

... OK. I'll see you later.

B 🔊 Check your answers with your class. Then listen again. **CD 2; Track 14**

What makes listening to English difficult? Many students think English speakers speak fast, but reducing structure words causes problems too.

Tell her she can sit here.

Tell ər she kən sit here.

Reducing words is a natural and normal part of the rhythm of English. Don't try to hear every word clearly. Pay more attention to the stressed words. You will be a more effective listener.

Notice

EXERCISE 2   **A** 🔊 Listen. Circle *a* or *b*. **CD 2; Track 15**

1. a. I'll **ask** for volun**teers** to **help**.
   b. I'll **ask four** volun**teers** to **help**.

2. a. It's **four** to **sev**en. (4:00 – 7:00)
   b. It's **four two seven**. (427)

3. a. They can **come** to the **par**ty.
   b. They **can't come** to the **par**ty.

4. a. The **pro**duct is for **eyes**.
   b. The **pro**duct is **Four Eyes**.

5. a. Is **this** to **clean**?
   b. Is **this too clean**?

6. a. It's on a **street** somewhere.
   b. It's on **A** Street somewhere.

B 🔊 Compare your answers with a partner. Then listen to both *a* and *b*. Can you hear a difference in rhythm? **CD 2; Track 16**

*"**No**, you want the **A** train. **This** is just a **train**."*

Rules and Practice

Reducing Structure Words

🔊 Listen to the pronunciation of the structure words alone. Then listen to them in a sentence. **CD 2; Track 17**

Alone: can /kæn/, you /yuʷ/, him /hɪm/, to /tuʷ/

In a sentence: Can you tell him   to   call me?
                /kn/ /yə/   /əm/   /tə/

RULE 10.1 Structure words are usually reduced in English. The vowel sounds often change to /ə/ or /ɪ/.

DID YOU **?**
KNOW

English speakers use full, clear forms of structure words when the structure word is:

- spoken alone: *to*
- at the end of a phrase: *Who are you writing to?*
- emphasized: *Don't take it from her; give it to her.*

Most of the time, however, structure words are reduced.

EXERCISE 3   **A** 🔊 Listen. Repeat the forms of the structure words and the examples. **CD 2; Track 18**

Common Structure Words

Full Form	Reduced Form	Example
1. a	/ə/	a book
2. and	/ən/, /ɪn/, /n/	soup and sandwich
3. as	/əz/	as busy as a bee
4. are	/ər/	The cookies are delicious.
5. can	/kən/, /kn/	I can go.
6. for	/fər/	It's for you.
7. have	/əv/, /v/, /ə/	What have you done?
8. her	/ər/	Give her the book.
9. him	/əm/, /ɪm/	Call him.
10. of	/əv/, /ə/*	all of us; cup of tea
11. or	/ər/	morning or afternoon
12. to	/tə/	We walk to school.

* Note: Use /əv/ before words that begin with vowel sounds: *all* /əv/ <u>us</u>. Use /ə/ before words that begin with consonant sounds: *cup* /ə/ <u>tea</u>.

B Write the structure words from part **A** that have these sounds when reduced.

1. /ə/ = ___a___ __have__ __of__   3. /ər/ = _____ _____ _____

2. /əv/ = _____ _____

EXERCISE 4 **A** 🔊 Listen and write the structure word you hear. CD 2; Track 19

1. I'd like the soup __and__ sandwich special.

2. I need a room _____ two nights.

3. I don't want the rest _____ my fries.

4. Could I talk _____ Farhad?

5. The phone's _____ you.

6. Let's go out _____ eat.

7. When _____ you graduating?

8. I want a bowl _____ soup.

9. He's going to Malaysia _____ Thailand.

10. Is he leaving on Monday _____ Tuesday?

B 🔊 Check your answers to part **A** with your class. Then listen again. CD 2; Track 19

C Work with a partner. Take turns saying the sentences.

EXERCISE 5 **A** Work with a partner. Complete each phrase with a word from the box.

coffee	**chips**	**ket**chup	~~**bread**~~	**milk**	**ce**real

1. **loaf** of _____bread_____

2. **pound** of _____

3. **bot**tle of _____

4. **quart** of _____

5. **box** of _____

6. **bag** of _____

B 🔊 Listen and check your answers. Repeat each phrase. CD 2; Track 20

C Work in a group. Take turns asking someone in the group: "What do we need from the store?" Remember to reduce the structure words.

> What do we need from the store?

> We need /ə/ **loaf** /ə/ **bread** and /ə/ **box** /ə/ **ce**real.

EXERCISE 6 **A** Work with a partner. Complete these popular dishes from around the world with the words in the box.

~~beans~~	**chips**	**hum**mus	**meat**balls
cabbage	**fries**	**jel**ly	**sal**sa

1. **rice** and _____beans_____

2. **bur**ger and _____

3. **fish** and _____

4. **pi**tas and _____

5. **chips** and _____

6. **pea**nut butter and _____

7. **corned beef** and _____

8. spa**ghet**ti and _____

B 🔊 Listen and check your answers in part **A**. Then listen and repeat. CD 2; Track 21

C Work in a group. Complete each sentence with a dish from part **A**.

1. In the Caribbean, _____rice and beans_____ is a common side dish.

2. Children in the U.S. like _____ for lunch.

3. In England, _____ is a popular meal.

4. In Middle Eastern countries, many people enjoy _____.

5. Everyone likes the classic Italian dish _____.

6. _____ is a popular Mexican appetizer.

7. A popular fast-food meal in the U.S. is a _____.

8. An Irish dish that many Americans enjoy on St. Patrick's Day is _____

_____.

D What is a popular food combination from your country? Tell your group about it.

Dropping /h/ in Structure Words

🔊 Listen. Notice what happens to the structure words *her* and *he*. CD 2; Track 22

Send ~~h~~er an application.   sounds like   *Sender* an application.
Will ~~h~~e tell the truth?   sounds like   *Willy* tell the truth?

RULE 10.2 When the structure words *her, he, him, his, have, has,* or *had* occur in the middle of a phrase, the *h* sound is often dropped.

EXERCISE 7 **A** 🔊 Listen to sentences with the reduced structure words *her*, *him*, *his*, and *he*.
CD 2; Track 23

1. She drove her car into a tree. She *drover* car into a tree.

2. Marta missed her bus again today. Marta *mister* bus again today.

3. Ang read his book all afternoon. Ang *readiz* book all afternoon.

4. Please ask her to call me. Please *asker* to call me.

5. Did you tell him to be on time? Did you *tellim* to be on time?

6. Is he on vacation? *Izzy* on vacation?

7. Was he sick? *Wuzzy* sick?

8. Did he get lost? *Diddy* get lost?

B Work with a partner. Practice saying the sentences.

EXERCISE 8 **A** Read the conversation. Cross out four more dropped *h* sounds.

A: The artist I like is showing his work at the museum. Do you want to go?

B: What's his name, again?

A: Yong Ho Ji. He's Korean. I learned about him in art class.

B: That's right! He creates animal sculptures. Doesn't he use old tires?

A: Yeah. They're amazing! Let's look at his website.

B 🔊 Listen and check your answers. CD 2; Track 24

C Work with a partner. Practice the conversation.

Can versus Can't

🔊 *Can* and *can't* are easily confused. What is the difference? Listen. CD 2; Track 25

You can **trust** him. (can = /kən/ or /kn/)

You **can't trust** him. (can't = /kænt/)

RULE 10.3 *Can* is usually reduced, or unstressed; the vowel sounds like /ə/ or is omitted. *Can't* is stressed; the vowel is a clear /æ/.

EXERCISE 9 **A** 🔊 Listen to a teacher telling students about their final project. Circle the word you hear: *can* or *can't*. CD 2; Track 26

1. Students (can / can't) work together.

2. Your project (can / can't) focus on topics we've studied in class.

3. If you aren't sure of a topic, you (can / can't) ask me, but I (can / can't) give you a topic.

4. Your project is due on the last day of class. You (can / can't) turn it in before then.

5. If you (can / can't) come to class, you (can / can't) give it to another student to hand in.

B 🔊 Listen again. Then take turns saying the sentences in part **A** with a partner. CD 2; Track 26

EXERCISE 10 **A** Find people in your class who *can* or *can't* do the following things. Walk around and ask your classmates: *Can you...?* Then write their names and circle *can* or *can't*.

1. _____ (can / can't) speak three languages.

2. _____ (can / can't) draw.

3. _____ (can / can't) play a musical instrument.

4. _____ (can / can't) play soccer.

5. _____ (can / can't) run a mile.

6. _____ (can / can't) fix cars.

7. _____ (can / can't) ski.

8. _____ (can / can't) sing.

9. _____ (can / can't) create a web page.

10. _____ (can / can't) fly a plane.

B Take turns sharing your answers with your class. Listen to your classmates. Nod your head *yes* if you hear *can*. Shake your head *no* if you hear *can't*.

○ ₒ ○
Gu /kn/ **cook.**

○ ○ ○
Ty can't cook.

A 🔊 Listen to the complete phone conversation from the Warm Up. Complete the sentences with the words you hear. **CD 2; Track 27**

A: Hi! _____ about **Mi**ka's gradu**a**tion party this **week**end?

B: **Yes. Mi**ka's **par**ty is on **Sun**day at her **house**.

A: _____ on **Col**lege Street?

B: That's **right**. It's **427**.

A: I'm a**fraid** _____ the **shop**.

B: I can **take** you.

A: **Great**! So, will there be _____?

B: **Yeah**. We're **hav**ing **cake** and **ice** cream.

A: Did you **ask** anyone _____?

B: I'll **ask** for volun**teers** to **help**.

A: What about **Vic**tor? _____?

B: **Vic**tor **can't come**, but he can **buy** the **gift**.

A: Sounds **good**. _____!

B: **OK**. I'll **see** you **la**ter.

B Check your answers with your class. Then work with a partner and practice the conversation.

C Work with another pair. Do a round robin reading—take turns reading each line.

A 🔊 A proverb is a saying that expresses a common belief. Listen and notice the rhythm and reduced words in each proverb. Then listen again and say each proverb with the speaker. CD 2; Track 28

Proverbs

1. **Live** and **learn**.

2. **No man** is an **is**land.

3. **Bet**ter **late** than **ne**ver.

4. **Two heads** are **bet**ter than **one**.

5. **Don't burn** your **brid**ges.

6. It **takes two** to **tan**go.

7. **Out** of **sight**, **out** of **mind**.

8. **Blood** is **thi**cker than **wa**ter.

9. You **can't judge** a **book** by its **co**ver.

10. You can **lead** a **horse** to **wa**ter, but you **can't make** him **drink**.

"HELLO, TOM! BETTER LATE THAN NEVER, EH?"

B Work with a partner. Match each proverb in part **A** with its meaning.

_____ It is better to do something late than not to do it at all.

___1___ It's natural to learn from our mistakes.

_____ If you can't see something, you won't think about it.

_____ When people work together, they think of better ideas.

_____ We need human connection.

_____ You can help someone and give them opportunities, but that person also has to make an effort to succeed.

_____ Things often look different than they are.

_____ Never leave situations with negative feelings.

_____ More than one person usually causes an argument.

_____ Family relationships are more important than other relationships.

C Circle your five favorite proverbs in part **A**. Then read them to your partner and say why you like them.

D Practice saying your favorite proverbs. When you are ready, record yourself saying them. Listen to the rhythm patterns. Re-record, if necessary. Then submit your recording to your teacher.

11 **Connected Speech**

OBJECTIVES

In this chapter, you will learn more about:

• how to link or connect words.

• how sounds get changed or lost when we connect words.

SUMMARY

In written English, we separate words. In spoken English, we connect words.

Written English: *What did you do?*

Spoken English: *Whadijado?*

The end of one word connects or links with the beginning of the next word. Words in a phrase might sound like one long word.

Warm Up

EXERCISE 1   **A**   Work with a partner. Read the conversation. It is written the way it sounds in *spoken* English. Write the conversation in *written* English.

Spoken English

A: Whadəyə do?

B: I-mə photographer.

A: Whadəyə take fodo-zəv?

B: Mostly family-zin pets.

A: Oh! Wou-jə tay-kə pictur-ə my family?

B: Shər.

Written English

A: What do you do? _____

B: _____

A: _____

B: _____

A: _____

B: _____

B 🔊 Check your answers with your class. Then listen to the conversation.
CD 2; Track 29

Notice

EXERCISE 2 **A** 🔊 Listen to each set of words. Do they sound the same or different? Check ✓ your answer. CD 2; Track 30

	Same	Different
1. major bed made your bed	✓	___
2. Andy won and he won	___	___
3. are often running are off and running	___	___
4. fairest of the mall fairest of them all	___	___
5. made a mistake made him a steak	___	___
6. a nice cold shower an ice cold shower	___	___
7. some mothers came some others came	___	___
8. didn't see Mable didn't seem able	___	___
9. needs a name needs an aim	___	___
10. the stuffy nose the stuff he knows	___	___

B 🔊 Share your answers to part **A** with your class. Then listen again. Notice that the words are different, but they sound the same. CD 2; Track 30

Rules and Practice

Linking: Final Consonant to Beginning Vowel

🔊 Words in a phrase are often linked, as you've seen in previous chapters. Listen. What happens when we link a final consonant sound to a beginning vowel sound? CD 2; Track 31

them all	Snow White is the fairest of them all.
an apple	May I have an apple, please?
walk away	Don't walk away!

RULE 11.1 When we link a final consonant to a beginning vowel sound, it sounds like the final consonant moves to the next word (for example, *them all* sounds like *the mall*).

EXERCISE 3   **A** 🔊 Listen. Repeat the phrases. CD 2; Track 32

1. Clean up. (Clea-nup.)
2. Work out. (Wor-kout.)
3. Turn off. (Tur-noff.)
4. Back up. (Bac-kup.)
5. Log off. (Lo-goff.)
6. What's up? (What-sup?)
7. Hold on! (Hol-don!)
8. Come in. (Co-min.)
9. Let's eat. (Let-seat.)
10. Open it. (Ope-nit.)

B Work with a partner. Take turns saying each phrase as one word.

EXERCISE 4   **A** 🔊 Draw a link from the underlined sounds to the vowel in the next word. Then listen to the conversation between two roommates. CD 2; Track 33

A: Hey, Jana, what's up?

B: Not much. I'm answering some emails. What's up with you?

A: Not too much. Do you want to walk over to campus with me?

B: Sure. Could you take a look at my essay first?

B With your partner, practice the conversation. Switch roles and practice again.

Linking: Final Consonant to Same Consonant

🔊 Listen. What happens when we link two consonant sounds that are the same? CD 2; Track 34

black coffee   I'll have a black coffee.

one night   He called one night last week.

weather report   What's the weather report?

RULE 11.2 When we link two consonant sounds that are the same, the consonant sound is pronounced once, not twice. The sound is a little longer.

EXERCISE 5

A 🔊 Close your eyes. Listen and repeat the phrases. CD 2; Track 35

bus stop	rock concert	speaks Spanish	watched TV
hot tea	some more	take care	wish she'd

B Work with a partner. Complete each sentence with a phrase from part **A**.

1. My friend got us tickets to a _rock concert_____.

2. Can you tell us where the closest _____ is?

3. Lucy is late again! I _____ be on time.

4. In the afternoon, I like to have a cup of _____.

5. Camilla _____ and Portuguese.

6. Last night I _____ and then went to bed.

7. May I have _____ coffee, please?

8. _____ of yourselves. See you again soon.

C 🔊 Check your answers with your class. Then listen and repeat each sentence. CD 2; Track 36

Linking and Sound Change: /t/ Between Vowels (*a lot of* = *alodda*)

🔊 What happens when /t/ comes between vowels? CD 2; Track 37

Within a word: *matter*   sounds like   *madder*

Between words: *a lot of*   sounds like   *a lodda*

RULE 11.3 When /t/ occurs between vowels and the second vowel is unstressed, the /t/ often sounds like a quick /d/.

EXERCISE 6   **A** 🔊 Listen to the conversations. Write the written form of the word or words to complete each conversation. **CD 2; Track 38**

1. A: Hurry up. We're late.

   B: Could you please _____wait_____ _____a_____ minute?

2. A: Did you get my message?

   B: Yes. I _____ _____ late last night. Thanks.

3. A: I'm _____ Lin for lunch. Do you want to come?

   B: No thanks. I'll see you _____.

4. A: It looks like rain.

   B: Yeah. You'd _____ take an umbrella.

5. A: _____ _____ you need from the store?

   B: Just _____ and _____.

6. A: Someday I'd like to _____ _____ book.

   B: I think you will! You're a good _____.

B 🔊 Work with a partner. Compare your answers. Then listen again to check them. **CD 2; Track 38**

C Practice the conversations in part **A** with your partner.

Linking and Sound Change: Final /d/+/y/

🔊 Listen. When a word ending in /d/ is followed by /y/, what *new* sound is formed? **CD 2; Track 39**

did you	What did you do over the weekend? (*did you = di-jə*)
read your	Can I read your essay? (*read your = rea-jər*)
would you	Would you get the door for me? (*would you = wou-jə*)

RULE 11.4 When we link a final /d/ to a beginning /y/, the two sounds form /dʒ/ as in *just*.

📍 **CHOOSE YOUR PATH**

• For pronunciation of /dʒ/ as in *just*, turn to Consonant Sounds 14, page 166.
• For practice linking /d/ to /y/, continue with the chapter.

EXERCISE 7   **A** 🔊 Listen. Do you hear the present or past? Circle the sentence you hear. **CD 2; Track 40**

1. (a.) They call you every day.

   b. They called you every day.

2. a. They always play your favorite song.

   b. They always played your favorite song.

3. a. I always pay your parking tickets.

   b. I always paid your parking tickets.

4. a. You dye your hair?

   b. You dyed your hair?

5. a. They owe you money, right?

   b. They owed you money, right?

6. a. Do you go to that gym on 2nd Avenue?

   b. Did you go to that gym on 2nd Avenue?

B 🔊 Check your answers with your class. Then listen to both sentences. Can you hear the difference between the present and the past? **CD 2; Track 41**

C Work with a partner. Student A, say sentence *a* or *b*. Student B, say *present* or *past*. Then switch roles.

EXERCISE 8 **A** 🔊 Listen and repeat these common question phrases. Notice the connected *d* + *y* sounds. **CD 2; Track 42**

Did you (Di-jə)   Would you (Wou-jə)   Could you (Cou-jə)

B 🔊 Listen. Write the question phrase from part **A** that you hear. **CD 2; Track 43**

1. Professor, _____ would you _____ mind if I leave a little early?

2. _____ open the door for me?

3. _____ take out the trash?

4. _____ help me?

5. _____ repeat that please?

6. Excuse me. _____ tell me where the train station is?

7. Wow! _____ see that bear?

8. It's dark. _____ get a flashlight?

C 🔊 Listen again and repeat each sentence. **CD 2; Track 44**

DID YOU KNOW ? It is not important for you to pronounce sound changes exactly the way native speakers do (e.g., *a lodda* for *a lot of*; *di-jə* for *did you*). It is more important to recognize these sound changes when you listen to English.

A 🔊 Listen and repeat the questions about manners in the United States. Write notes about your ideas. **CD 2; Track 45**

1. What should you do when you meet someone for the first time?

   shake hands, introduce yourself, say "nice to meet you"

2. When should you arrive at a friend's house for a party?

   _____

3. What should you do when you accidentally bump into someone?

   _____

4. If you do not want any more food, what should you say?

   _____

5. If a dress code is "business casual," what should you wear?

   _____

B Work with a partner. Take turns asking and answering the questions in part **A**.

C Report your answers to your class. Discuss any questions that you did not know the answers to.

D In a group or as a class, take turns asking and answering the questions again. This time, answer based on customs in your country or culture.

A 🔊 Listen to these common idioms. Notice the connected speech as you repeat them. **CD 2; Track 46**

Idiom	Sounds like
How's it going?	*How-zit going?*
Keep an eye on it.	*Kee-pi-neye o-nit.*
Let's call it a day.	*Let's ca-li-də day.*
… make up your mind.	*Ma-kəp your mind.*
Get to the point.	*Ge-tə the point.*
… get on my nerves.	*… ge-don my nerves*
I get it.	*I ge-dit.*
… see eye to eye.	*… see eye-də eye*
You've got to be kidding.	*You've go-də be kidding.*
Would you like a hand?	*Wou-jə li-kə hand?*

B With a partner, write the idiom from part **A** next to the phrase with the same or similar meaning.

1. My neighbors <u>bother me</u>.   My neighbors <u>get on my nerves</u>.
2. We don't <u>agree</u>.   We don't _____.
3. Let's <u>stop working</u>.   Let's _____.
4. You're <u>not serious</u>.   _____.
5. <u>Watch this closely</u>.   _____.
6. Tell him to <u>tell the story faster</u>.   Tell him to _____.
7. <u>Do you want help</u>?   _____?
8. <u>I understand</u>.   _____.
9. Please <u>decide</u>.   Please _____.
10. <u>How's your life</u>?   _____?

C 🔊 Listen and check your answers to part **B**. **CD 2; Track 47**

D Practice saying the sentences in part **B** with a partner. Monitor your partner's connected speech. When you are ready, record yourself saying them. Listen to your connected speech. Re-record, if necessary. Then submit your recording to your teacher.

TIP ▼ Songs and Connected Speech

To improve your listening skills, look up the lyrics to your favorite songs online. Listen to the song and practice saying or singing the lyrics. This will help you with connected speech and rhythm.

PART V Discourse: Focus, Intonation, and Thought Groups

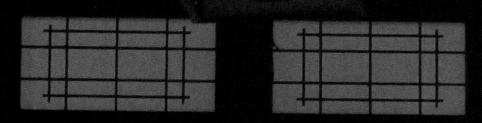

Guests talk in a room at Ankokuji Temple in Hyogo, Japan.

OBJECTIVES

In this chapter, you will learn:

- what a focus word is.
- how focus words are pronounced.
- which words are focus words, and why.

SUMMARY

You have learned about the basic rhythm of English, which is the pattern of strong beats and weak beats. The strong beats occur on stressed words, which are usually content words. In every phrase or sentence, one of the stressed words is stronger than the others. This is the focus word. The focus word is the most important word in the phrase or sentence. It provides new or special information.

Warm Up

EXERCISE 1 **A** Work with a partner. Compare the colleges below. Underline the differences.

- <u>public</u> college
- two-year college
- in a large city
- 29,000 students (20% international)
- tuition: $6,000 per semester

- <u>private</u> college
- four-year college
- in a small city
- 1,000 students (6% international)
- tuition: $26,000 per semester

B Discuss which college you would prefer. Why?

"The college in Maine has a better <u>curri</u>culum, but the
college in New York has better **pi**zza."

EXERCISE 2 **A** 🔊 Listen. Pay attention to the <u>underlined</u> words. CD 2; Track 48

1. Linwood is **pub**lic. Walton is **pri**vate.

2. Linwood is a **two**-year college, and Walton is a **four**-year college.

B 🔊 Did you notice anything different about the underlined words? Listen again.
CD 2; Track 48

EXERCISE 3 **A** 🔊 Listen. Underline the word in each sentence that is stressed the most.
CD 2; Track 49

1. Linwood is located in a <u>large</u> city. Walton is in a small city.

2. Linwood's tuition is six thousand a semester. Walton's is twenty-six thousand.

B 🔊 Check your answers with your class. Then listen again. CD 2; Track 49

EXERCISE 4 **A** 🔊 Listen to the speaker hum these sentences. What makes the underlined words
stand out? CD 2; Track 50

1. Linwood has a **huge** population, but Walton has a **small** one.

2. Walton's tuition is <u>ex**pen**sive</u>. Linwood's is more af**ford**able.

B 🔊 Discuss your answer with your class. Did you hear the pitch of the voice
change on the underlined words? Listen again. CD 2; Track 50

<table>
<tr><td>DID YOU KNOW ?</td><td>In this chapter, you will be listening to pitch changes on focus words. What is pitch? Well, just as songs have high notes and low notes, speech has high pitches and low pitches. English speakers use pitch jumps to highlight important words.</td></tr>
</table>

Rules and Practice

Focus Words

The focus word is the most important word in each phrase or sentence.

I graduated from **Wal**ton. My major was engi**nee**ring.

RULE 12.1 Normally, the focus word is the last content word in a phrase or sentence.

Hearing the Focus Word

You learned that structure words are unstressed and content words are stressed. The focus word, however, is stressed or emphasized the most.

🔊 Listen. What makes the focus word stand out? CD 2; Track 51

I've finished **col**lege. My major was engi**nee**ring.

RULE 12.2 The vowel in the focus word (or in the stressed syllable of the focus word) is long and clear. Most important, however, is that the pitch of the voice jumps on the focus word.

EXERCISE 5

A Work with a partner. Underline the last content word in each sentence. This is the focus word.

1. When did you <u>call</u>?
2. When did you call me?
3. I brought my notes.
4. I brought my notes for you.

5. The teacher is nice.
6. The teacher is nice to us.
7. The server was rude.
8. The server was rude to her.

B 🔊 Check your answers with your class. Then listen and repeat each sentence in part **A**. Notice the pitch jump on the focus words. CD 2; Track 52

EXERCISE 6 **A** How do you manage stress in your life? Choose five of your favorite "stress busters." Rank them from 1 to 5 in the third column.

Stress Busters	Example	Mine	My Partner's
1. listen to **mu**sic	2		
2. read a **book**			
3. watch **te**levision	5		
4. go to the **mo**vies			
5. take a **nap**			
6. talk to my **fa**mily			
7. work out at the **gym**			
8. take a **walk**	3		
9. do **yo**ga	1		
10. go **shop**ping			
11. take a hot **bath**	4		
12. hang out with **friends**			
Other:			

B Work with a partner. Share your answers to part **A**. Be sure to make the focus word in each phrase stand out. Write your partner's ranking in the last column.

> How do you manage
> **stress**?

> I do **yo**ga. I also like
> to …

Special Focus: New Information

🔊 Focus can change from the last content word. It can move to other important words for special reasons. Listen to the special focus on the word *elementary* in line B. **CD 2; Track 53**

A: Miguel's major was edu**ca**tion.

B: Right. Ele**men**tary education.

RULE 12.3 Use focus to highlight new information.*

*Note: Keep old information at a low pitch so new information will stand out.

Special Focus: Answering *Wh-* Questions

🔊 Listen to the special focus on the word *Raj* in line B. CD 2; Track 54

A: Who told you about my new **job**?

B: **Raj** told me about it.

RULE 12.4   Use focus to highlight answers to *wh-* questions.

TIP ▼ Pronunciation

As you say the focus word, add one of these movements:

• Stretch a rubber band.
• Nod your head slightly.
• Raise your eyebrows.

Wake **up**!   I hear a **noise**!

EXERCISE 7   **A** 🔊 Listen to these conversations. CD 2; Track 55

Conversation 1

A: Wake **up**! I hear a **noise**!

B: What **kind** of noise?

A: A **scra**tching noise. I'm really a**fraid**!

B: It's probably the **cat**. Go back to **sleep**.

Conversation 2

A: What are you **watch**ing?

B: A **mo**vie.

A: A **sca**ry movie?

B: Yes, a **ve**ry scary movie!

B Work with a partner. Practice the conversations in part **A**. Make the focus words jump out. Raise your eyebrows, nod your head, or stretch a rubber band as you say each underlined focus word.

EXERCISE 8 **A** With a partner, underline the focus word in each sentence.

Conversation 1

A: Let's order a <u>pizza</u>.

B: But I'm on a diet.

A: Maybe you can break your diet.

Conversation 2

A: I'll see you on Thursday.

B: I'm off on Thursday.

A: Oh, when do you return?

B: On Friday.

Conversation 3

A: Let's go to Italy.

B: But we don't have the money.

A: Maybe we could borrow the money.

B Check your answers with your class. Then listen to the conversations. CD 2; Track 56

C Work with a new partner. Practice the conversations in part **A**. Make the focus words jump.

Special Focus: Making Corrections

Listen to speaker B correct speaker A. Notice the special focus on the word *three*. CD 2; Track 57

A: So, you've completed two years of **col**lege.

B: Actually, **three** years.

RULE 12.5 Use focus to highlight a correction.

EXERCISE 9 **A** Work with a partner. Read A's lines. Then look at the Warm Up on page 95 and write the correction in line B. The correction is the focus word.

1. A: Linwood is **pri**vate.

   B: No, it's _____public_____.

2. A: Linwood is in a small **ci**ty.

   B: No, it's in a _____ city.

3. A: I think you can go to Linwood for four **years**.

   B: No, only _____ years.

4. A: Somebody told me that Linwood has about 39,000 **stu**dents.

   B: Actually, it has _____ students.

5. A: I heard that fifty percent of Linwood's students are inter**na**tional.

   B: No, it's _____ percent.

6. A: My friend said that the tuition at Linwood is ex**pen**sive.

   B: Well, compared to Walton, it's _____ .

B With your partner, practice the short conversations in part **A**. Make the focus words jump out.

Linwood is **pri**vate.   No, it's **pub**lic.

Special Focus: Contrasting Information

🔊 Listen. Notice the special focus on the words *large* and *small*. CD 2; Track 58

Linwood College is in a **large** city, and Walton is in a **small** city.

RULE 12.6 Use focus to highlight contrasting information.

EXERCISE 10 **A** Work with a partner. Complete the sentences with the words from the box.

Africa	**Asia**	**East**	**Po**land	**two-year**
apple	**coo**kie	**four**-year	the **Czech** Re**pub**lic	**West**

1. Linwood is a _____two-year_____ college, whereas Walton is a

   _____ college.

2. Prague is in _____ , not in _____ .

3. Indonesia is in _____ , and Kenya is in _____ .

4. New York City is on the _____ Coast, and Los Angeles is on the

   _____ Coast.

5. An _____ is better for you than a _____ .

B 🔊 Listen and check your answers. Then listen again and say the sentences with the speaker. CD 2; Track 59

📍 **CHOOSE YOUR PATH**

- For practice with focus words and vowel sounds, read the Tip in Vowel Sounds 1, page 122, and do the exercises on page 123.
- For practice with focus words and specific vowel sounds, see Exercise 6 in Vowel Sounds 4–7.
- For communicative practice, continue with the chapter.

A Work with a partner. Read the incorrect facts about world events in the twentieth century. Write the correction in line B. Guess if you aren't sure of the answer.

How much do you know about the twentieth century?

1. A: The *Titanic* was built in 1912.

   B: Actually, the *Titanic* <u>sank</u> in 1912.

2. A: World War I ended in 1945.

   B: I think you mean World War _____ ended in 1945.

3. A: North Korea and South Korea became one country after World War II.

   B: I think you mean that they became _____ countries after World War II.

4. A: The first person walked on Mars in 1969.

   B: You mean that the first person walked on the _____ in 1969.

5. A: Germans put up the Berlin Wall in 1989.

   B: Wait, Germans took _____ the Berlin Wall in 1989, right?

6. A: Brazil has won the World Cup seven times.

   B: Are you sure? I think Brazil has won only _____ times.

B Work with your class. Take turns reporting the incorrect and corrected statements. Remember that your correction is the focus word.

> The *Titanic* was built in 19**12**.

> Actually, the *Titanic* **sank** in 1912.

C 🔊 Listen and say the conversations with the speakers. Half of the class says A's lines, and the other half says B's lines. **CD 2; Track 60**

D With your partner, write three more *incorrect* facts. Then take turns sharing them with your class. Ask your classmates to correct you.

1. _____

2. _____

3. _____

Pronunciation Log | Focus Words

A 🔊 Listen to the statements in part **B**. Who is speaking? Who is each person speaking to? **CD 2; Track 61**

B Work with a partner. Take turns saying the statements. Pronounce the focus words fully and clearly. Then, together, write something else that each person might say.

At school

Ex**cuse** me. I have a question about my **quiz**. Number four is marked **wrong**, but I think it's **right**.

Excuse me. I have a question about

At a shoe store

I'd like to exchange these **shoes**. I need a size **nine**, not a size **ten**.

I'd like to return

At work

I think there's a mis**take**. Last **week**, I worked twenty-**nine** hours, but I was paid for twenty-**five**.

I'd like to ask you about

C Underline the focus words in your statements. Then share one or more of your statements with your class. Make sure your teacher checks your focus marks.

D Practice saying the lines. When you are ready, record yourself saying both the model statements and your statements. Listen and monitor your pronunciation of the focus words. Re-record if necessary. Then submit your recording to your teacher.

CHAPTER 13 Final Intonation

OBJECTIVES

In this chapter, you will learn:

- how the voice rises or falls at the end of sentences.
- about intonation patterns in statements and questions.

SUMMARY

Intonation is the change in tune or pitch of the voice. You learned that the voice usually jumps on the focus word (the most important word) in each phrase. Then the voice **rises** ↗ or **falls** ↘. Most sentences end with a rising or falling intonation.

A: Did you lock the **door**? ↗

B: Where are the **keys**? ↘

A: I don't **know**. ↘

Warm Up

EXERCISE 1   **A**   Work with a partner. You want to find out whether your partner would be a good roommate. Take turns asking and answering the questions.

> ### Roommate Wanted
> to Share Great Apartment
> Near Campus!
>
> $500 / private room with shared bath. Laundry, heat/water included. Near transportation!

Yes/No Questions

1. Do you watch TV?

2. Do you stay up late?

3. Are you neat?

4. Do you like cats?

Wh- Questions

5. When do you usually go to bed?

6. What time do you get up?

7. Where do you live now?

8. Why are you moving?

B   Did your voice rise ↗ or fall ↘ at the end of these questions? Tell your class.

Notice

EXERCISE 2   **A** 🔊 Listen to this conversation, which has only one word per line. Notice how the voice either rises or falls at the end of each word. Circle ↘ if the voice falls and ↗ if it rises. **CD 2; Track 62**

	Falls	**Rises**
A: Cold?	↘	(↗)
B: No.	(↘)	↗
A: Tired?	↘	↗
B: Yes.	↘	↗
A: Why?	↘	↗
B: Roommate.	↘	↗
A: Roommate?	↘	↗
B: Yes.	↘	↗
A: Student?	↘	↗
B: Musician.	↘	↗
A: Pianist?	↘	↗
B: Drummer.	↘	↗

B 🔊 Check your answers with your class. Then listen again. **CD 2; Track 62**

EXERCISE 3   **A** 🔊 Listen. Draw a ↘ if the voice falls at the end of the question. Draw a ↗ if the voice rises at the end. **CD 2; Track 63**

1. What's your name?   ↘   5. Do you have a car?   _____

2. Where did you grow up?   _____   6. Do you like pets?   _____

3. When do you eat dinner?   _____   7. Do you play an instrument?   _____

4. What are your hobbies?   _____   8. Are you a night owl?   _____

B 🔊 Check your answers with your class. Listen again. Did you hear a difference between the *wh-* questions and the *yes/no* questions? **CD 2; Track 63**

Rules and Practice

Falling Intonation: Statements

🔊 Listen. Notice the intonation at the end of the statements. **CD 2; Track 64**

We're looking for a **room**mate. ↘

Daniel has a **car**. ↘

RULE 13.1 In statements, the voice usually jumps up on the focus word and then begins to fall.

Falling Intonation: *Wh-* Questions

🔊 Listen. Notice the intonation at the end of the *wh-* questions. **CD 2; Track 65**

A: What **year** are you? ↘   B: A senior.

A: When is your gradu**a**tion? ↘   B: At the end of May.

RULE 13.2 In *wh-* questions that ask for new information, the voice usually jumps up on the focus word and then begins to fall.

EXERCISE 4   **A** 🔊 Listen and repeat the questions. Draw a ↘ at the end. **CD 2; Track 66**

1. Where are you **li**ving? ↘

2. Why are you **stu**dying?

3. Where did you grow **up**?

4. What do you typically eat for **din**ner?

5. When do you usually go to **bed**?

6. What do you like to do in your free **time**?

B Work with a partner. Take turns asking and answering the questions from part **A**.

Where are you **li**ving? ↘   In a **dorm**. ↘

C With your partner, write three *wh-* questions to ask your teacher. Mark the final intonation.

1. _____

2. _____

3. _____

D With your class, take turns asking your teacher your questions from part **C**.

> What time do you usually wake up? ↘
>
> I usually wake up around 6:00. ↘

Rising Intonation: *Yes/No* Questions

🔊 Listen. Notice the intonation at the end of the *yes/no* question. **CD 2; Track 67**

A: Are you a **stu**dent? ↗
B: Yes. At State University.

RULE 13.3 In *yes/no* questions, the voice usually jumps on the focus word and then rises.

EXERCISE 5

A 🔊 Listen and repeat the questions. Draw a ↗ at the end. **CD 2; Track 68**

1. Do you have a **car**? ↗

2. Do you have a **job**?

3. Do you like **cats**?

4. Are you living in a **dorm**?

5. Are you a **mor**ning person?

6. Have you ever had a bad **room**mate?

B Work with a partner. Take turns asking and answering the questions from part **A**.

> Do you have a **car**? ↗
>
> No, I don't. ↘

C With your partner, write three *yes/no* questions to ask your teacher. Mark the final intonation.

1. _____

2. _____

3. _____

D With your class, take turns asking your teacher your questions from part **C**.

TIP ▼ Returned Questions

When English speakers first meet, they often return the same question. Here is a returned *wh-* question.

> A: Where are you from?
>
> B: Morocco. *Where are you from?*

Returned questions are also common in everyday speech. Here is a returned *yes/no* question.

> A: Did you study for the quiz?
>
> B: A little. *Did you study?*

Focus and Intonation in Returned Questions

🔊 Listen. Notice the focus word and the final intonation in the returned question.
CD 2; Track 69

A: What do you **do**? ↘
B: I'm a student. What do **you** do? ↘

RULE 13.4 In returned questions, the focus word changes, but the final intonation stays the same.

EXERCISE 6 **A** Work with a partner. Mark the final intonation of the questions with a ↘ or a ↗.

1. What's your **name**? ↘

2. Do you play **sports**?

3. When did you **move** here?

4. Do you like living in this **town**?

5. Where are you **from**?

6. Do you **work**?

7. What do you do in your free **time**?

8. How was your **week**end?

B With your partner, take turns asking and answering the questions in part **A**. When you answer a question, return it. Be sure to use the correct final intonation.

What's your **name**? ↘   Peter. What's **your** name? ↘

Lu. Do you play **sports**? ↗   No. Do **you**? ↗

Communicative Practice | Roommates

A 🔊 Listen to the complete conversation from the beginning of the chapter. Mark the final intonation with a ↗ or a ↘. **CD 2; Track 70**

A: Are you **cold**? ↗

B: **No**. ↘

A: Are you **tired**?

B: Yes, I'm **rea**lly tired.

A: **Why**?

B: Because of my **room**mate.

A: Your **room**mate?

B: Yes.

A: Is your roommate a **stu**dent?

B: No, she's a mu**si**cian.

A: Is she a **pi**anist?

B: No, she's a **drum**mer.

B 🔊 Check your answers to part **A** with your class. Then listen again. **CD 2; Track 70**

C Work with a partner. Complete the conversation using your own ideas. Mark the final intonation.

A: Are you _____?

B: No.

A: Are you _____?

B: Yes, I'm really _____.

A: Why?

B: Because of my roommate.

A: Your roommate?

B: Yes.

A: Is your roommate _____

_____?

B: No, _____.

A: Is _____?

B: No, _____.

© John McPherson/Distributed by Universal Uclick via CartoonStock.com 9-8

LAST NIGHT THERE WERE 93 TISSUES IN MY TISSUE BOX AND NOW THERE ARE ONLY 89!

UNIV OF MICH

Holly gets off to a rough start with her new roommate.

D With your partner, practice the conversation. Then take turns sharing your conversation with your class.

A Work with a partner. Read the questions people commonly ask landlords. Mark the final intonation with a ↗ or a ↘.

1. How much is the **rent**? ↘

2. How long is the **lease**?

3. What is your policy on **pets**?

4. Can I have a **cat**?

5. How much is the de**po**sit?

6. Is the neighborhood **safe**?

7. Does the apartment get **sun**light?

8. Is there a **dish**washer?

9. Can I walk to the **gro**cery store?

10. Does the rent include u**til**ities?

11. Is there **par**king?

12. Is the apartment close to public transpor**ta**tion?

> **Roommate Wanted**
> to Share Great Apartment
> Near Campus!
>
> **$500** / private room with shared bath. Laundry, heat/water included.Near transportation!

B 🔊 Listen and check your answers from part **A**. Repeat each sentence.
CD 2; Track 71

C Circle the five questions from part **A** that you think are most useful. Then, with your partner, take turns asking and answering your questions. Pretend you are a landlord when you are answering. Monitor your partner's final intonation.

Can I have a **cat**? ↗   Yes, but there's a $400 deposit for cats. ↘

D When you are ready, record yourself asking your five questions. Listen and monitor your final intonation. Re-record if necessary. Then submit your recording to your teacher.

CHAPTER 14 Thought Groups

OBJECTIVES

In this chapter, you will learn:
* what a thought group is.
* how to identify thought groups.
* how thought groups help listeners understand meaning.

SUMMARY

Speakers divide language into phrases called *thought groups.* Thought groups are groups of words that go together to express an idea or thought. Each thought group usually has one strongly stressed focus word and a brief pause at the end. Using thought groups makes your speech easier to understand. It also makes you sound more fluent.

If you'd like to make a **call**, / please hang **up** / and dial a**gain**.

Warm Up

EXERCISE 1   **A** 🔊 Listen to this message on Juan's office phone. Mark each break or pause with a /. **CD 2; Track 72**

> You have reached Juan Rodriguez / at Global Technologies I'm not at my desk
>
> right now so please leave a message and I'll return your call as soon as I can

B 🔊 Check your answers with your class. Then listen again. **CD 2; Track 72**

Notice

EXERCISE 2   **A** 🔊 Close your eyes. Listen to the speaker say the same sentence two different ways. **CD 2; Track 73**

1. This is a terrible connection so let's hang up and I'll call you right back.
2. This is a terrible con**nec**tion / so let's hang **up** / and I'll call you right **back**.

B Work with a partner. Discuss which sentence in part **A** was easier to understand. Why?

EXERCISE 3   **A** 🔊 Read both sentences. Then listen and circle the sentence you hear.
CD 2; Track 74

    1. a. Larisa said, "Ivan got a great new job."

       b. "Larisa," said Ivan, "got a great new job."

    2. a. James thinks Joseph will get a promotion.

       b. James, thinks Joseph, will get a promotion.

    3. a. Jun made breakfast quickly, ate it, and went to work.

       b. Jun made breakfast, quickly ate it, and went to work.

B 🔊 Check your answers with your class. Then listen to both sentences.
CD 2; Track 75

C With a partner, discuss the differences in meaning between sentences *a* and *b* in part **A**.

Rules and Practice

Thought Groups

🔊 Listen to the thought groups in this sentence. CD 2; Track 76

I'm **so**rry / but I'm **sick** / and I can't come to **work** today.

RULE 14.1 A thought group is a group of words that naturally go together. A thought group forms a logical thought or idea.*

*Note: Each thought group usually has one focus word.

EXERCISE 4   **A** Work with a partner. Decide which thought groups make more sense. Circle *a* or *b*.

    1. a. I don't exercise because I work / too much.

      (b.) I don't exercise / because I work too much.

    2. a. It was a long day / with many meetings.

      b. It was a long / day with many meetings.

    3. a. Could we change the meeting / to another time?

      b. Could we change the meeting to / another time?

    4. a. I lost / my ID badge / and have to get a new one.

      b. I lost my ID badge / and have to get a new one.

    5. a. I didn't recognize / Jorge after he shaved off his beard.

      b. I didn't recognize Jorge / after he shaved off his beard.

B 🔊 Check your answers with your class. Then listen and repeat the correct sentence in each pair. CD 2; Track 77

EXERCISE 5   **A** Write one thought group to complete each sentence starter.

1. After I **ex**ercise, _____ .

2. When I start **wor**king, _____ .

3. If you don't like the service in a **re**staurant, _____ .

4. The best gift I ever re**ceived** _____ .

5. After **En**glish class, _____ .

B Work with a partner. Take turns saying your sentences.

> After I **ex**ercise, I feel **great**.

Thought Groups and Pausing

In writing, we use commas and other punctuation to show where thought groups end.

Your office, which is on the fourth floor, has a window.

🔊 Listen. How do we show where thought groups end in speaking?
CD 2; Track 78

Your office / which is on the fourth floor / has a window.

RULE 14.2 Speakers often pause briefly at the end of a thought group.

Thought Groups and Intonation

We also use the rise and fall of our voice, or intonation, to signal the end of a thought group.

🔊 Listen. CD 2; Track 79

I'm really **sorry**, / but I have a flat **tire**, / so I'm going to be **late**.

RULE 14.3 The voice jumps on the focus word and then falls slightly at the end of each thought group. Then the intonation falls more at the end of the sentence.

EXERCISE 6 **A** Match the thought groups. Then practice saying the sentences. Use pauses and intonation to mark the thought groups.

1. Sorry to **bo**ther you, __c__   a. you should take a **ta**xi.

2. As far as I **know**, ___   b. about the best **per**son for the **job**.

3. Let's make a de**ci**sion ___   c. but where did you put my **note**book?

4. If I earned a higher **sa**lary, ___   d. we don't have to **work** this weekend.

5. To be **safe**, ___   e. I would buy a **house**.

B 🔊 Listen and check your answers. Then listen and say the sentences with the speaker. **CD 2; Track 80**

Thought Groups: Numbers and Letters

🔊 Listen to the way that these numbers and letters are grouped. **CD 2; Track 81**

U.S. telephone number:	(404) / 555 / 8648
U.S. Social Security or ID number:	943 / 33 / 3211
Address:	2489 / Channel Center Street / Suite 100
	Boston / MA / 02210
Email address:	darasmith / @smithcat / .com
URL:	www / .spca914 / .com

RULE 14.4 Thought groups can also be groups of letters or numbers. We pause at specific places in common fixed numbers or letters.

EXERCISE 7 **A** 🔊 Listen. Mark the end of each thought group with a /. **CD 2; Track 82**

1. 976/53/2297

2. 3533 Conley Road Suite 200

3. Rockwall Texas 75087

4. April 23 1982

5. 3105554441

6. www.favoritepoem.org

7. tomkatz@mymail.com

B 🔊 Check your answers with a partner. Then listen again and repeat. **CD 2; Track 83**

A Write your name, address, phone number, and email address below (or create an imaginary person). Mark the end of each thought group.

Job Application

Name: _____

Address: _____

_____

_____

Phone number: _____

Email address: _____

B Imagine that you have an interview for your dream job. Complete the sentence.

I'm the right person for this job because _____ .

C Work with a partner. Dictate the information from parts **A** and **B** to your partner. Write your partner's information in the form.

My Partner's Information

Name: _____

Address: _____

_____

_____

Phone number: _____

Email address: _____

I'm the right person for this job because _____

D Check your answers with your partner.

TIP ▼ Spelling and Thought Groups

When spelling out words for people, it's helpful to divide the word into syllables.

My last name is Anderson. That's A-N / D-E-R / S-O-N.

Pronunciation Log | Thought Groups

A 🔊 Listen to a voicemail message to Juan at Global Technologies from Jill, who is interested in a job. Then listen again and say the message with Jill. CD 2; Track 84

> Hi **Juan**. / My name is Jill **Yang**. / I'm calling about the computer **pro**gramming position. / I'm very **in**terested / and would love to discuss my ex**per**ience. / I can be reached by **e**mail / at jill**yang** / **@me** / .**com** / or by **phone** / at 5**55**- / 2**32**- / 4**036**. / I look forward to **hear**ing from you.

B With a partner, take turns practicing the message from Jill to Juan.

C When you are ready, record yourself reading the message. Listen and monitor your pronunciation of thought groups. Re-record if necessary. Then submit your recording to your teacher.

PART VI Vowel and Consonant Sounds

**Waiters on break at a hotel
in New Orleans, USA**

1 Vowel Overview

OBJECTIVE

In this overview, you will learn about the differences between English vowel sounds.

SUMMARY

When we make vowel sounds, the air flows freely. We do not block the air with the lips, teeth, or tongue. We do, however, change the size and shape of the mouth to make different vowel sounds. This section will help you see how and where to make vowel sounds.

Notice

EXERCISE 1   **A** Look at the diagrams. Notice where each vowel sound is made in the mouth.

Where in the mouth are the vowel sounds made?

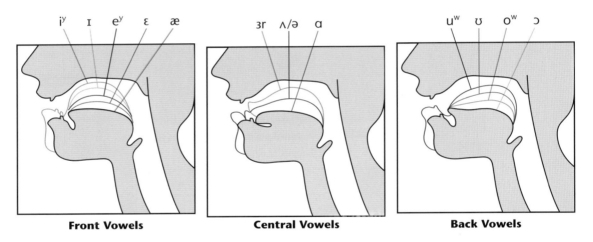

Front Vowels   **Central Vowels**   **Back Vowels**

B 🔊 Listen to the vowel sounds, starting at the top of each diagram. Repeat each sound silently as you listen. Notice how your tongue and lips move. **CD 3; Track 2**

C 🔊 Listen again and repeat each sound. Circle the sounds that are challenging for you. **CD 3; Track 2**

Practice

Vowel Chart

We make different vowel sounds by changing the position of the tongue, jaw, and lips. The location of each vowel sound on the chart below shows the tongue and lip position for that vowel in relation to other vowel sounds.

🔊 Listen and repeat each sound and example word in the chart. **CD 3; Track 3**

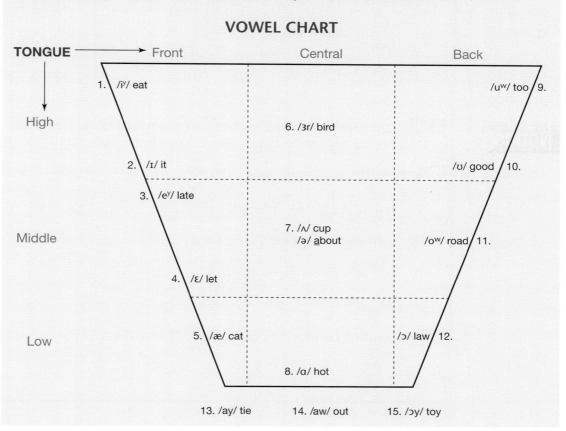

VOWEL CHART

TONGUE ⟶ Front   Central   Back

High
- 1. /iʸ/ eat
- 6. /ɜr/ bird
- 9. /uʷ/ too
- 2. /ɪ/ it
- 10. /ʊ/ good
- 3. /eʸ/ late

Middle
- 7. /ʌ/ cup /ə/ about
- 11. /oʷ/ road
- 4. /ɛ/ let

Low
- 5. /æ/ cat
- 12. /ɔ/ law
- 8. /ɑ/ hot

13. /ay/ tie   14. /aw/ out   15. /ɔy/ toy

EXERCISE 2

A Circle the correct answers. Look at the Vowel Chart for help.

1. a. Say /iʸ/ as in *he*. Your tongue is at the ((front)/ back) of your mouth.

   b. Say /uʷ/ as in *too*. Your tongue is at the (front / back) of your mouth.

2. a. Put your hands on your cheeks. Say /iʸ/ as in *he*. Your lips are (spread / rounded).

   b. Put your hands on your cheeks. Say /uʷ/ as in *too*. Your lips are (spread / rounded).

3. a. Put your hand on your chin. Say /ɑ/ as in *hot*. Your tongue and jaw are (high / low).

   b. Put your hand on your chin. Say /iʸ/ as in *he*. Your tongue and jaw are (high / low).

B Look again at the Vowel Chart. Notice that the location of each vowel sound in the chart relates to the location of your tongue when you make the sound.

Front Vowels

The front of the tongue starts high in the mouth. The tongue and jaw move down as you say the front vowels. The lips are spread.

🔊 Listen to the front vowels and example words. CD 3; Track 4

/iʸ/ see
/ɪ/ sit
/eʸ/ say
/ɛ/ said
/æ/ sad

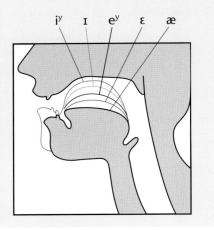

EXERCISE 3 **A** 🔊 Listen and repeat the sounds and example words. Notice the position of the tongue for each sound in the Front Vowels diagram. CD 3; Track 5

1. /iʸ/ - he, these, leaf, feed, _____

2. /ɪ/ - hit, sick, win, miss, pin, _____

3. /eʸ/ - may, rain, paint, late, same, _____

4. /ɛ/ - get, yes, red, jet, send, _____

5. /æ/ - mad, sad, man, bag, pan, _____

B Work with a partner. Say each word. Then write it in the correct place in part **A**.

mess	hat	with	tree	wake

Central Vowels

The tongue is in the center of the mouth for these sounds.

For /ʌ/ and /ə/, the tongue and jaw are higher than for /ɑ/.

For /ʌ/, /ə/, and /ɑ/, the lips are in a neutral position; they are not spread or rounded. For /ɜr/, the lips round slightly.

🔊 Listen to the central vowels and example words. CD 3; Track 6

/ɜr/ work
/ʌ/ up, ab<u>o</u>ve
/ə/ <u>a</u>bove
/ɑ/ stop

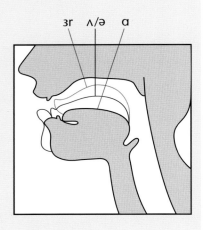

EXERCISE 4

A 🔊 Listen and repeat the sounds and example words. Notice the position of the tongue for each sound in the Central Vowels diagram. CD 3; Track 7

1. /ɜr/ - bird, her, nurse, work, _____

2. /ʌ/ - cup, truck, gum, run, _____

3. /ə/ - around, sof<u>a</u>, a, the, _____

4. /ɑ/ - hot, stop, job, shop, _____

B Work with a partner. Say each word. Then write it in the correct place in part **A**.

| hurt | Americ<u>a</u> | socks | bug |

Back Vowels

The back of the tongue starts high in the mouth for /uʷ/. As you say the remaining back vowels, the tongue and jaw move down. The lips are rounded.

🔊 Listen to the back vowels and example words. CD 3; Track 8

/uʷ/ two
/ʊ/ good
/oʷ/ know
/ɔ/ call

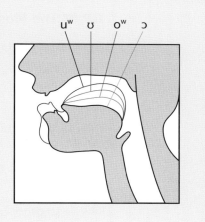

EXERCISE 5

A 🔊 Listen and repeat the sounds and example words. Notice the position of the tongue for each sound in the Back Vowels diagram. CD 3; Track 9

1. /uʷ/ - too, food, choose, rule, suit, _____

2. /ʊ/ - good, book, pull, full, should, _____

3. /oʷ/ - know, soap, home, joke, phone, _____

4. /ɔ/ - law, long, ball, caught, walk, _____

B Work with a partner. Say each word. Then write it in the correct place in part **A**.

| boss | toe | moon | could |

Diphthongs

Diphthongs begin with a vowel sound (/a/ or /ɔ/) and move through a second sound (/w/ or /y/). Symbols for the three diphthongs vary in dictionaries, but in *Well Said* we use the following symbols.

🔊 Listen to the diphthongs and example words. CD 3; Track 10

/ay/ rice   /aw/ cow   /ɔy/ boy

EXERCISE 6 **A** 🔊 Listen and repeat the sounds and words. CD 3; Track 11

1. /ay/ - fine, white, light, sky, tie, _____

2. /aw/ - now, house, south, brown, _____

3. /ɔy/ - void, toy, noise, join, _____

B Work with a partner. Say each word. Then write it in the correct place in part **A**.

joy   eye   ab<u>ou</u>t

TIP ▼ The Most Important Vowel in Words and Phrases

The most important vowel in a word is the one in the syllable with the **primary stress**.

     /æ/   /ɛ/
un der **stand** No **vem** ber

The most important vowel in a phrase or sentence is the stressed vowel in the **focus word**.*

   /uʷ/   /ɑ/
I'm a **<u>stu</u>** dent. I study bi **o** lo <u>gy</u>.

Be sure to pronounce vowel sounds in stressed syllables clearly, especially vowel sounds in focus words.

---

*Note: See Chapter 11 to learn more about focus words.

EXERCISE 7 **A** Circle the correct vowel sound for each stressed syllable.

1. be**gin**   (/ɪ/) or /ɛ/   4. **dir**ty   /ɜr/ or /iʸ/

2. con**fuse**   /ʊ/ or /uʷ/   5. No**vem**ber /iʸ/ or /ɛ/

3. Ja**pan**   /æ/ or /eʸ/   6. four**teen** /iʸ/ or /ay/

B 🔊 Listen and repeat the words from part **A**. Make the stressed vowels full and clear. **CD 3; Track 12**

EXERCISE 8 **A** Work with a partner. Write the correct symbol from the box above the stressed syllable of each underlined focus word. Each sound is used once.

/iʸ/ see	/ɛ/ said	/ɜr/ work	/oʷ/ go
/ɪ/ sit	/æ/ sad	/uʷ/ pool	/ɑ/ stop
/eʸ/ say	/ʌ/ ab<u>o</u>ve	/ʊ/ should	~~/ɔ/ ball~~

                              /ɔ/
A: Did you just **call** me?

B: Yes.

A: What's the **mat**ter?

B: I don't know what to wear to **school**.

A: Just throw on a **shirt**.

B: But **which** shirt?

A: A **tee** shirt.

B: My **red** tee shirt, my **gray** tee shirt, my **con**cert tee shirt, my **Lon**don tee shirt, …?

A: I don't **know**! They all look **good**. You decide!

B 🔊 Listen to the conversation. Then practice it with a partner. **CD 3; Track 13**

Glided Vowels

Four vowels glide or move toward a second sound. That is why these sounds have a second symbol: /ʸ/ or /ʷ/. Many languages do not have glided vowels, so you may not notice the difference between glided and non-glided vowels in English. The primary difference is mouth movement. When you say a non-glided vowel, there is no mouth movement. When you say a glided vowel, the mouth and tongue move toward the second sound.

🔊 Listen to these sounds and example words. CD 3; Track 14

Glided	Non-Glided
/iʸ/ sleep	/ɪ/ slip
/eʸ/ late	/ɛ/ let
/uʷ/ Luke	/ʊ/ look
/oʷ/ low	/ɔ/ law

DID YOU KNOW ?

If you confuse glided and non-glided vowels, you could be misunderstood. For example:

/iʸ/		/ɪ/
She's _leaving_ there.	might sound like	She's _living_ there.
/eʸ/		/ɛ/
I need some _paper_.	might sound like	I need some _pepper_.

EXERCISE 9   **A** 🔊 Listen and repeat the pairs of sounds. CD 3; Track 15

Glided	Non-Glided
/iʸ/	/ɪ/
/eʸ/	/ɛ/
/uʷ/	/ʊ/
/oʷ/	/ɔ/

B Your teacher will say the sound pairs in part **A** silently, without sound. Can you _see_ the difference between the glided and non-glided vowels?

C 🔊 Listen and repeat these sounds and words. CD 3; Track 16

Glided	Non-Glided		Glided	Non-Glided
1. /iʸ/ sleep	/ɪ/ slip		5. /uʷ/ Luke	/ʊ/ look
2. /iʸ/ leave	/ɪ/ live		6. /uʷ/ pool	/ʊ/ pull
3. /eʸ/ late	/ɛ/ let		7. /oʷ/ low	/ɔ/ law
4. /eʸ/ taste	/ɛ/ test		8. /oʷ/ boat	/ɔ/ bought

2 Vowel Sounds and Spelling

OBJECTIVE

In this vowel lesson, you will learn about common sound-spelling relationships.

SUMMARY

English sounds are represented in writing in a variety of ways, often based on the origin of the word. Learning common patterns will help you predict the pronunciation of a word.

Vowel Sounds and Spelling

Vowels that sound like the alphabet letters (A, E, I, O, and U) are spelled in different ways. Here are some common spelling patterns for these sounds.

A /e^y/: *a...e, ai, ay, eigh*   O /o^w/: *o...e, oa, ow, oe*

E /i^y/: *e...e, ea, ee*   U /u^w/: *u...e, ue, ew, oo*

I /ay/: *i...e, igh, ie, y*

EXERCISE 1   **A** Work with a partner. Take turns reading the example words. Try to add one more word to each spelling pattern.

Letter	Sound	Spelling Patterns	Examples
A	/e^y/	a...e ai ay	cake, sale, make nail, rain, day, way,
E	/i^y/	e...e ea ee	scene, Pete, seat, read, teen, bee,
I	/ay/	i...e igh ie y	fine, lime, tight, night, tie, pie, my, try,
O	/o^w/	o...e oa ow oe	phone, home, boat, coal, blow, crow, toe, Joe,
U	/u^w/	u...e ue ew oo	tune, use, due, Sue, few, new, soon, boot,

B Share your answers to part **A** with your class. Which spelling pattern(s) were more difficult to find words for?

EXERCISE 2 **A** Homophones are words that sound the same but have different spellings. With a partner, write a homophone for each word.

1. /uʷ/ blue: _____blew_____

2. /eʸ/ eight: _____

3. /oʷ/ no: _____

4. /eʸ/ male: _____

5. /iʸ/ peace: _____

6. /ʌ/ sun: _____

7. /uʷ/ threw: _____

8. /uʷ/ to: _____

9. /eʸ/ wait: _____

10. /ʊ/ wood: _____

B Find the homophones that you wrote in part **A** in the Word Search. Check your spelling.

Word Search

i	t	u	p	i	e	c	e	u	n	t
w	o	c	r	n	o	w	i	q	y	h
k	n	o	w	l	f	z	w	y	t	r
a	r	e	o	o	b	l	e	w	h	o
a	u	w	u	m	q	b	i	v	r	u
m	a	i	l	a	l	a	g	i	a	g
t	l	s	d	e	k	a	h	i	u	h
f	g	t	f	l	h	a	t	e	t	f
u	a	w	f	b	g	o	r	o	h	u
l	s	o	n	r	f	i	z	y	i	l

3 What vowel sounds should you study?

OBJECTIVE

This page will help you identify some important vowel sounds to study.

SUMMARY

English vowel sounds that do not occur in your language may be challenging for you to hear or say. The activity below will help you choose vowel sounds that you need to practice.

Selecting Vowel Sounds to Study

A 🔊 Listen to these sound pairs. If it is hard to hear the difference, one of the sounds may be difficult for you. Go to the vowel lesson for practice.
CD 3; Track 17

1. /iʸ/   don't h**ea**t it
   /ɪ/   don't h**i**t it   ☐ Easy   ☐ Hard   → *See Vowels 4, p. 128*

2. /eʸ/   a bad p**ai**n
   /ɛ/   a bad p**e**n   ☐ Easy   ☐ Hard   → *See Vowels 5, p. 132*

3. /æ/   he s**a**t
   /ɛ/   he s**e**t   ☐ Easy   ☐ Hard   → *See Vowels 6, p. 136*

4. /ʌ/   my l**u**ck
   /ɑ/   my l**o**ck   ☐ Easy   ☐ Hard   → *See Vowels 7, p. 140*

B Look at your Pronunciation Needs Form in Chapter 1 on page 5. Did your teacher note vowel sounds that were difficult for you to say? Write the sounds and one or two example words.

_____

_____

_____

4 /iʸ/ _sh**ee**p_ - /ɪ/ _sh**i**p_

OBJECTIVE

In this vowel lesson, you will learn to perceive and produce /iʸ/ and /ɪ/.

SUMMARY

Many students have difficulty hearing the distinction between /iʸ/ and /ɪ/. They may say _sheep_ for _ship_ or _ship_ for _sheep_. These sounds are important because there are many pairs of words in English, such as _leave/live,_ that differ only by these sounds.

Notice

EXERCISE 1   🔊 Listen to the sounds /iʸ/ (as in _sheep_) and /ɪ/ (as in _ship_). Notice the difference.
CD 3; Track 18

/iʸ/ ... /ɪ/ ... /iʸ/ ... /ɪ/ ... /iʸ/ ... /ɪ/ ... /iʸ/ ... /ɪ/

EXERCISE 2   **A** 🔊 Listen to the word pairs with /iʸ/ and /ɪ/. **CD 3; Track 19**

1. cheek - chick	3. heel - hill	5. leave - live	7. sleep - slip
2. eat - it	4. leap - lip	6. reach - rich	8. team - Tim

B 🔊 Listen to the word pairs. This time, some words are the same. If the words are the same (_cheek - cheek_), write S. If the words are different (_cheek - chick_), write D.
CD 3; Track 20

1. _S_   3. ___   5. ___   7. ___

2. ___   4. ___   6. ___   8. ___

C 🔊 Check your answers to part **B** with your class. Then listen again.
CD 3; Track 20

Practice

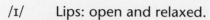

Pronouncing /iʸ/ and /ɪ/

/iʸ/	Lips: spread.
	Tongue: tense and high in the mouth.
	The front of the tongue glides up and forward slightly as you say the sound.
	Note: /iʸ/ says the letter name *E*.

/ɪ/	Lips: open and relaxed.
	Tongue: relaxed and high, but not as high as for /iʸ/.
	The tongue does not move.

Note: Common spellings for /iʸ/ are: -ee (*seen*); -ea (*meat*); -e-e (*these*); -e (*me*).
The most common spelling for /ɪ/ is: -i- (*big*).

EXERCISE 3 🔊 Listen again. Repeat each sound after the speaker. **CD 3; Track 21**

/iʸ/ … /ɪ/ … /iʸ/ … /ɪ/ … /iʸ/ … /ɪ/ … /iʸ/ … /ɪ/

EXERCISE 4 **A** 🔊 Listen to the word pairs again. Repeat each word pair. **CD 3; Track 22**

1. cheek - chick	3. heel - hill	5. leave - live	7. sleep - slip
2. eat - it	4. leap - lip	6. reach - rich	8. team - Tim

B Circle a, b, or c. Take turns reading the word pair you circled to a partner. Write the word pair your partner says. Do not let your partner see your book.

<table>
<tr><th colspan="3" style="text-align:center">Your Word Pairs</th><th style="text-align:center">Your Partner's
Word Pairs</th></tr>
<tr><td>1. a. cheek - chick</td><td>b. chick - chick</td><td>c. cheek - cheek</td><td>_____ - _____</td></tr>
<tr><td>2. a. it - it</td><td>b. eat - eat</td><td>c. eat - it</td><td>_____ - _____</td></tr>
<tr><td>3. a. leave - leave</td><td>b. leave - live</td><td>c. live - live</td><td>_____ - _____</td></tr>
<tr><td>4. a. reach - rich</td><td>b. rich - rich</td><td>c. reach - reach</td><td>_____ - _____</td></tr>
</table>

C Check your answers with your partner. Then tell your class how you did.

EXERCISE 5 **A** 🔊 Listen to the speaker say sentence *a* or *b*. Check ✓ the matching response.
CD 3; Track 23

1. a. Did you feel it?   ✓ Yes, it's cold.

   b. Did you fill it?   ____ Yes, it was empty.

2. a. He wants to leave there. ____ I know. He doesn't like it.

   b. He wants to live there.   ____ Yes, he likes it.

3. a. That's my team.   ____ You play a sport?

   b. That's my Tim.   ____ You have a son?

4. a. Did you sleep?   ____ Yes, I was tired.

   b. Did you slip?   ____ Yes, I hurt my arm.

B 🔊 Check your answers with your class. Then listen and repeat both sentences and responses. CD 3; Track 24

C Work with a partner. Look again at the sentences in part **A**. Student A, say sentence *a* or *b*. Student B, say the matching response. Then switch roles.

EXERCISE 6 **A** 🔊 Listen and repeat the words. They are the focus words (or key words) in the conversation in part **B**. CD 3; Track 25

/iʸ/: **leave**, **eat**, **cheese**, **eat**en, **seen**, **cheap**

/ɪ/: **Mick's**, ter**ri**fic, con**vinced**

B 🔊 Listen to the conversation. Notice the stress on the focus words. Then listen again. Half the class says line A *with* the speaker. The other half says line B. CD 3; Track 26

Lunchtime

A: Are you ready to **leave**?

B: Yeah, let's **eat**.

A: How about **Mick's**? They have the best mac and **cheese**.

B: I've never **eat**en there. I've never even **seen** it!

A: Well, the food's ter**ri**fic, and it's **cheap**.

B: Okay! You've con**vinced** me.

C Practice the conversation in part **B** with a partner. Switch roles and practice again.

EXERCISE 7 **A** 🔊 Listen to the paragraph. Notice the pronunciation of the /iʸ/ and /ɪ/ sounds in the highlighted words. **CD 3; Track 27**

Counting Sheep

Many people have trouble falling asleep. Some try to count sheep. They believe they will get tired if they repeat the same thing over and over again. Therefore, they visualize sheep jumping over a fence, one after the other. They simply *bore* themselves to sleep!

"Yes, she always falls asleep when she does the daily attendance count."

B Work with a partner. Write each highlighted word from part **A** in the correct column.

/iʸ/ (as in *feet*)	/ɪ/ (as in *fit*)
people	

C 🔊 Check your answers with your class. Then listen to the paragraph again. **CD 3; Track 27**

D Practice reading *Counting Sheep*. When you are ready, record yourself. Listen and monitor your pronunciation of the highlighted words. Re-record if necessary. Then submit your recording to your teacher.

5 /eʸ/ l<u>a</u>te - /ɛ/ l<u>e</u>t

OBJECTIVE

In this vowel lesson, you will learn to perceive and produce /eʸ/ and /ɛ/.

SUMMARY

Many students have difficulty hearing the distinction between /eʸ/ and /ɛ/. They may say *late* for *let* or *let* for *late*. These sounds are important because there are many pairs of words in English, such as *pen/pain* and *wait/wet*, that differ only by these sounds.

Notice

EXERCISE 1 🔊 Listen to the sounds /eʸ/ (as in *late*) and /ɛ/ (as in *let*). Notice the difference.
CD 3; Track 28

/eʸ/ ... /ɛ/ ... /eʸ/ ... /ɛ/ ... /eʸ/ ... /ɛ/ ... /eʸ/ ... /ɛ/

EXERCISE 2 **A** 🔊 Listen to the word pairs with /eʸ/ and /ɛ/. CD 3; Track 29

1. wait - wet	3. date - debt	5. main - men	7. l<u>a</u>ter - l<u>e</u>tter
2. pain - pen	4. taste - test	6. whale - well	8. age - edge

B 🔊 Listen to the word pairs. This time, some words are the same. If the words are the same (*wait - wait*), write *S*. If the words are different (*wait - wet*), write *D*.
CD 3; Track 30

1. <u>D</u>   3. ___   5. ___   7. ___

2. ___   4. ___   6. ___   8. ___

C 🔊 Check your answers to part **B** with your class. Then listen again.
CD 3; Track 30

Practice

Pronouncing /eʸ/ and /ɛ/

/eʸ/:   Lips: spread and tense.

Tongue: tense and positioned in the middle part of your mouth.

The front part of the tongue moves up and forward as you say the sound.

Note: /eʸ/ sounds like the letter name *A*.

/ɛ/:   Lips: open, relaxed, and slightly spread.

Tongue: relaxed and a little lower than for /eʸ/.

The tongue does not move.

Note: Common spellings for /eʸ/ are: a-e (*late, shape*); -ai, (*rain, mail*); -ay (*day, gray*).
The most common spelling for /ɛ/ is: -e- (*pen, tent*).

EXERCISE 3   🔊 Listen again. Repeat each sound after the speaker. **CD 3; Track 31**

/eʸ/ … /ɛ/ … /eʸ/ … /ɛ/ … /eʸ/ … /ɛ/ … /eʸ/ … /ɛ/

EXERCISE 4   **A** 🔊 Listen to the word pairs again. Repeat each word pair. **CD 3; Track 32**

1. wait - wet	3. date - debt	5. main - men	7. later - letter
2. pain - pen	4. taste - test	6. whale - well	8. age - edge

B Circle a, b, or c. Take turns reading the word pair you circled to a partner. Write the word pair your partner says. Do not let your partner see your book.

Your Word Pairs			**Your Partner's Word Pairs**
1. a. wait - wet	b. wait - wait	c. wet - wet	_____ - _____
2. a. pain - pain	b. pen - pen	c. pen - pain	_____ - _____
3. a. test - taste	b. test - test	c. taste - taste	_____ - _____
4. a. edge - age	b. age - age	c. edge - edge	_____ - _____

C Check your answers with your partner. Then tell your class how you did.

EXERCISE 5

A 🔊 Listen to the speaker say sentence *a* or *b*. Check ✓ the matching response.
CD 3; Track 33

1. a. Do you have any dates?   _____ No, I'm staying home.

    b. Do you have any debts?   ✓ No, I've never borrowed money.

2. a. I have a terrible pain.   _____ Call your doctor.

    b. I have a terrible pen.   _____ You can borrow mine.

3. a. Was that your first taste?   _____ Yes, it was delicious.

    b. Was that your first test?   _____ Yes, it was easy.

4. a. Where's the paper?   _____ Aisle 2, with office supplies.

    b. Where's the pepper?   _____ Aisle 5, with spices.

B 🔊 Check your answers with your class. Then listen and repeat both sentences and responses. CD 3; Track 34

C Work with a partner. Look again at the sentences in part **A**. Student A, say sentence *a* or *b*. Student B, say the matching response. Then switch roles.

EXERCISE 6

A 🔊 Listen and repeat the words. They are the focus words (or key words) in the conversation in part **B**. CD 3; Track 35

/eʸ/: **great**, **aged**, **shape**, **day**, **train**er, **weight**

/ɛ/: **Jen**, **Ben**, for**e**ver, **help**

B 🔊 Listen to the conversation. Notice the stress on the focus words. Then listen again. Half the class says line A *with* the speaker. The other half says line B.
CD 3; Track 36

Long Time, No See

A: Hey **Jen**! You look **great**! You've barely **aged**!

B: Thanks, **Ben**! Wow, it's been for**e**ver!

A: It has. So, tell me, how do you stay in such great **shape**?

B: Well, I work out every **day**. And I'm a personal **train**er now.

A: Oh, well I need to lose **weight**. Can you **help**?

C Practice the conversation in part **B** with a partner. Switch roles and practice again.

EXERCISE 7 **A** 🔊 Listen to the following statements. Notice the pronunciation of the /eʸ/ and /ɛ/ sounds in the highlighted words. Then tell your class whether you think each statement is a fact or a myth. **CD 3; Track 37**

Fact or Myth?

1. You can't fold a piece of paper in half more than seven times.

2. The heart of a blue whale is as big as a car.

3. Women say more words per day than men.

4. You lose more heat from your head than any other part of your body.

5. You can gain weight if you get less than seven hours of sleep a night.

B Work with a partner. Write each highlighted word from part **A** in the correct column.

/eʸ/ (as in *late*)	/ɛ/ (as in *let*)
paper	

C 🔊 Check your answers with your class. Then listen to the statements again. **CD 3; Track 37**

D Practice reading *Fact or Myth*? When you are ready, record yourself. Listen and monitor your pronunciation of the highlighted words. Re-record if necessary. Then submit your recording to your teacher.

6 /æ/ b<u>a</u>d - /ɛ/ b<u>e</u>d

OBJECTIVE
In this vowel lesson, you will learn to perceive and produce /æ/ and /ɛ/.

SUMMARY
Many students have difficulty hearing the distinction between /æ/ and /ɛ/. They may say *bad* for *bed* or *bed* for *bad*. These sounds are important because there are many pairs of words in English, such as *man / men*, that differ only by these sounds.

Notice

EXERCISE 1 🔊 Listen to the sounds /æ/ (as in *man*) and /ɛ/ (as in *men*). Notice the difference.
CD 3; Track 38

/æ/ ... /ɛ/ ... /æ/ ... /ɛ/ ... /æ/ ... /ɛ/ ... /æ/ ... /ɛ/

EXERCISE 2 **A** 🔊 Listen to the word pairs with /æ/ and /ɛ/. CD 3; Track 39

1. bad - bed	3. sad - said	5. sat - set	7. salary - celery
2. man - men	4. mass - mess	6. laughed - left	8. taxes - Texas

B 🔊 Listen to the word pairs. This time, some words are the same. If the words are the same (*bed - bed*), write S. If the words are different (*bad - bed*), write D.
CD 3; Track 40

1. _S_   3. ____   5. ____   7. ____

2. ____   4. ____   6. ____   8. ____

C 🔊 Check your answers to part **B** with your class. Then listen again.
CD 3; Track 40

Practice

> **Pronouncing /æ/ and /ɛ/**
>
> /æ/:   Lips: open wide and slightly spread.
>   Tongue: low and forward.
>
> /ɛ/:   Lips: open, relaxed, and slightly spread.
>   Tongue: relaxed and a little lower than for /eʸ/.
>   The tongue does not move.

Note: The most common spelling for /æ/ is: -a- (*mat, bad*).
The most common spelling for /ɛ/ is: -e- (*met, bed*).

EXERCISE 3   🔊 Listen again. Repeat each sound after the speaker. CD 3; Track 41

/æ/ … /ɛ/ … /æ/ … /ɛ/ … /æ/ … /ɛ/ … /æ/ … /ɛ/

EXERCISE 4   **A** 🔊 Listen to the word pairs again. Repeat each word pair. CD 3; Track 42

1. bad - bed	3. sad - said	5. sat - set	7. salary - celery
2. man - men	4. mass - mess	6. laughed - left	8. taxes - Texas

B Circle a, b, or c. Take turns reading the word pair you circled to a partner. Write the word pair your partner says. Do not let your partner see your book.

<table>
<tr><td align="center" colspan="3">Your Word Pairs</td><td align="center">Your Partner's
Word Pairs</td></tr>
<tr><td>1. a. men - men</td><td>b. men - man</td><td>c. man - man</td><td>_____ - _____</td></tr>
<tr><td>2. a. said - sad</td><td>b. said - said</td><td>c. sad - sad</td><td>_____ - _____</td></tr>
<tr><td>3. a. mass - mass</td><td>b. mess - mess</td><td>c. mess - mass</td><td>_____ - _____</td></tr>
<tr><td>4. a. laughed - left</td><td>b. left - left</td><td>c. laughed - laughed</td><td>_____ - _____</td></tr>
</table>

C Check your answers with your partner. Then tell your class how you did.

EXERCISE 5

A 🔊 Listen to the speaker say sentence *a* or *b*. Check ✓ the matching response. CD 3; Track 43

1. a. I saw the man.   ✓ Where is he now?

   b. I saw the men.   ___ Where are they now?

2. a. They left.   ___ Where did they go?

   b. They laughed.   ___ Was it that funny?

3. a. The celery is good.   ___ Yes, it's very fresh.

   b. The salary is good.   ___ How much money is it?

4. a. I hate taxes.   ___ Me too!

   b. I hate Texas.   ___ Why? It's a great state!

B 🔊 Check your answers with your class. Then listen and repeat both sentences and responses. CD 3; Track 44

C Work with a partner. Look again at the sentences in part **A**. Student A, say sentence *a* or *b*. Student B, say the matching response. Then switch roles.

EXERCISE 6

A 🔊 Listen and repeat the words. They are the focus words (or key words) in the yoga instructions in part **B**. CD 3; Track 45

/æ/: **class**, re**lax**, **hands**, **mat**, **stand**, **back**

/ɛ/: **Beth**, **breath**, **head**, **stretch**, a**gain**, **legs**

B 🔊 Listen to the yoga instructor. Notice the stress on the focus words. Then listen again. Repeat the instructions. CD 3; Track 46

Yoga Class

"Hello **class**. My name is **Beth**.

First, let's just sit and re<u>**lax**</u>. Take a deep **breath** . . .

Now, take two more, and with each breath, raise your **hands** above your

head. **Stretch**. Then release your breath and bring your hands to your **mat**.

A**gain** . . .

OK. Now please **stand**. Inhale, and raise your arms over your **head**. Exhale,

and fold over your **legs**. Inhale and straighten your **back**. Exhale . . ."

C Practice saying the instructions in part **B** with a partner.

EXERCISE 7   **A** 🔊 Listen to these strange laws. Notice the pronunciation of the /æ/ and /ɛ/ sounds in the highlighted words. CD 3; Track 47

Strange Laws

1. In A<u>la</u>ska, you cannot wake up a bear to take a picture with it.
2. In C<u>a</u>lifornia, you cannot s<u>e</u>t a mousetrap unless you g<u>e</u>t a hunting license.
3. In Mi<u>a</u>mi, Florida, it is illegal to imitate an <u>a</u>nimal.
4. In Kentucky, people must take a b<u>a</u>th at least once a year.
5. In M<u>a</u>ssachusetts, you cannot put tomatoes in cl<u>a</u>m chowder.*
6. In New York, it is illegal to throw a ball at a person's h<u>ea</u>d for fun.
7. In Washington state, you cannot pret<u>e</u>nd your parents are rich.
8. In W<u>e</u>st Virginia, only babies can ride in a baby carriage.

"All right, on three everybody snarl."

Clam chowder is a type of seafood soup.

B Work with a partner. Write each highlighted word from part **A** in the correct column.

/æ/ (as in *bad*)	/ɛ/ (as in *bed*)
Alaska	

C 🔊 Check your answers with your class. Then listen again. CD 3; Track 47

D Practice reading *Strange Laws*. When you are ready, record yourself. Listen and monitor your pronunciation of the highlighted words. Re-record if necessary. Then submit your recording to your teacher.

7 /ʌ/ c<u>u</u>p - /ɑ/ c<u>o</u>p

OBJECTIVE

In this vowel lesson, you will learn to perceive and produce /ʌ/ and /ɑ/.

SUMMARY

Many students have difficulty hearing the distinction between /ʌ/ and /ɑ/. They may say *cup* for *cop* or *cop* for *cup*. These sounds are important because there are many pairs of words in English, such as *luck/lock*, that differ only by these sounds.

Notice

EXERCISE 1   🔊 Listen to the sounds /ʌ/ (as in *cut*) and /ɑ/ (as in *hot*). Notice the difference.
CD 3; Track 48

/ʌ/ ... /ɑ/ ... /ʌ/ ... /ɑ/ ... /ʌ/ ... /ɑ/ ... /ʌ/ ... /ɑ/

EXERCISE 2   **A** 🔊 Listen to the word pairs with /ʌ/ and /ɑ/. CD 3; Track 49

1. hut - hot	3. luck - lock	5. duck - dock	7. color - collar
2. nut - not	4. rub - rob	6. buddy - body	8. done - Don

B 🔊 Listen to the word pairs. This time, some words are the same. If the words are the same (*hut - hut*), write S. If the words are different (*hut - hot*), write D.
CD 3; Track 50

1. __S__   3. ____   5. ____   7. ____

2. ____   4. ____   6. ____   8. ____

C 🔊 Check your answers to part **B** with your class. Then listen again.
CD 3; Track 50

Practice

Pronouncing /ʌ/ and /ɑ/

/ʌ/   Lips: Slightly open and relaxed; neither rounded nor spread.

       Tongue: Relaxed.

/ɑ/   Lips: Open and relaxed; neither rounded nor spread.

       Tongue: Relaxed; tongue and jaw are lower than for any other vowel sound.

       Note: This is the sound you make when the doctor wants to look in your throat.

Note: Common spellings for /ʌ/ are: -u- (*bus, much*); -o- (*month, love, won, some, mother*).

The most common spelling for /ɑ/ is: -o- (*hot, stop*).

*In some accents in the United States and Canada, there is little difference between /ɔ/*caught* and /ɑ/ *cot.*

EXERCISE 3 🔊 Listen again. Repeat each sound after the speaker. CD 3; Track 51

     /ʌ/ ... /ɑ/ ... /ʌ/ ... /ɑ/ ... /ʌ/ ... /ɑ/ ... /ʌ/ ... /ɑ/

EXERCISE 4 **A** 🔊 Listen to the word pairs again. Repeat each word pair. CD 3; Track 52

1. hut - hot	3. luck - lock	5. duck - dock	7. c<u>o</u>lor - c<u>o</u>llar
2. nut - not	4. rub - rob	6. b<u>u</u>ddy - b<u>o</u>dy	8. done - Don

B Circle a, b, or c. Take turns reading the word pair you circled to a partner. Write the word pair your partner says. Do not let your partner see your book.

<table>
<tr><th colspan="3" align="center">Your Word Pairs</th><th align="center">Your Partner's
Word Pairs</th></tr>
<tr><td>1. a. nut - nut</td><td>b. not - not</td><td>c. not - nut</td><td>_____ - _____</td></tr>
<tr><td>2. a. lock - lock</td><td>b. luck - lock</td><td>c. luck - luck</td><td>_____ - _____</td></tr>
<tr><td>3. a. rub - rob</td><td>b. rob - rob</td><td>c. rub - rub</td><td>_____ - _____</td></tr>
<tr><td>4. a. collar - collar</td><td>b. color - color</td><td>c. collar - color</td><td>_____ - _____</td></tr>
</table>

C Check your answers with your partner. Then tell your class how you did.

EXERCISE 5 **A** 🔊 Listen to the speaker say sentence *a* or *b*. Check ✓ the matching response. CD 3; Track 53

1. a. Whose hut?   ✓ Ours.

 b. Who's hot?   ___ I am.

2. a. Is that a duck?   ___ No, it's a goose.

 b. Is that a dock?   ___ Yes, it's for our boat.

3. a. My buddy is tired.   ___ He should rest.

 b. My body is tired.   ___ You should rest.

4. a. He just shut the door. ___ Okay, great. Let's go.

 b. He just shot the door. ___ Oh no! Why?

B 🔊 Check your answers with your class. Then listen and repeat both sentences and responses. CD 3; Track 54

C Work with a partner. Look again at the sentences in part **A**. Student A, say sentence *a* or *b*. Student B, say the matching response. Then switch roles.

EXERCISE 6 **A** 🔊 Listen and repeat the words. They are the focus words (or key words) in the conversation in part **B**. CD 3; Track 55

/ʌ/: **bus, what, fun, lunch, luck**

/ɑ/: **not, for**got**, top, lot**

B 🔊 Listen to the conversation. Notice the stress on the focus words. Then listen again. Half the class says line A *with* the speaker. The other half says line B. CD 3; Track 56

Fun Run

A: I have to go catch the **bus**.

B: For **what**?

A: Did you forget? Today I'm doing that ***fun*** run.

B: You mean we aren't having **lunch**?

A: No, we're **not**.

B: Sorry, I for**got**! Well, good **luck**! I'm sure you'll come out on **top**!

A: Thanks a **lot**.

C Practice the conversation in part **B** with a partner. Switch roles and practice again.

EXERCISE 7

A 🔊 Listen to the paragraph. Notice the pronunciation of the /ʌ/ and /ɑ/ sounds in the highlighted words. **CD 3; Track 57**

Origin of the Name *Hot Dog*

Where did we get the name *hot dog*? The *hot* part is <u>o</u>bvious. Sausages are hot. In fact, sausages are too hot to hold, so a baker invented the b<u>u</u>n. The *dog* part is n<u>o</u>t as obvious. They say that in the mid-1800s, people were afraid sausage makers were using dog meat. Therefore, the name *hot dog* came about, and somehow, the name st<u>u</u>ck! The first record of the word was in 1893, in the *Kn<u>o</u>xville Journal*, a newspaper in Iowa. Since then, hot dogs have bec<u>o</u>me as American as baseball and apple pie.

B Work with a partner. Write each highlighted word from part **A** in the correct column.

/ʌ/ (as in *luck*)	/ɑ/ (as in *lock*)
	hot

C 🔊 Check your answers with your class. Then listen again. **CD 3; Track 57**

D Practice reading *Origin of the Name Hot Dog*. When you are ready, record yourself. Listen and monitor your pronunciation of the highlighted words. Re-record if necessary. Then submit your recording to your teacher.

8 Consonant Overview

OBJECTIVE

In this overview, you will learn about the differences between English consonant sounds.

SUMMARY

Three main features of consonant sounds can create challenges for students.

- **Voicing:** The difference between voiceless and voiced sounds can create confusion. For example, students may say _be_ for _pea_ or _tack_ for _tag_.
- **Airflow:** Whether the air slows down or stops completely is also important. For example, when we say /t/, the air stops and is then released. When we say /s/, the air slows down (_ssss_).
- **Place:** Where the air stops or slows is another important aspect of consonant sounds in English. Seeing pictures of the mouth and practicing sounds will help you learn how English sounds are made.

Notice

EXERCISE 1 **A** 🔊 Listen to the sounds. Notice that the first sound in each pair is voiceless and the second is voiced. **CD 4; Track 2**

1. /k/ - /g/   2. /t/ - /d/   3. /f/ - /v/   4. /s/ - /z/

B 🔊 Now listen and repeat the pairs of sounds. Notice the placement of your tongue, lips, and mouth. Each pair of sounds in part **A** is pronounced in the same place. The only difference is the voicing. **CD 4; Track 3**

> **DID YOU KNOW ?** English has eight consonant pairs that are _almost_ alike. We say the sounds in each pair the same way, except that one is voiceless and the other is voiced. For example, /p/ is voiceless and /b/ is voiced. Say _pie_ and _bye_. The only difference between /p/ and /b/ is the voicing.

Voicing: *Is the sound voiceless or voiced?*

Voiceless and Voiced Consonant Sounds

🔊 Place your hand on your throat. Listen and repeat. CD 4; Track 4

s-s-s-s-s-s

z-z-z-z-z-z

Consonant sounds are either voiceless or voiced. When you say voiceless sounds like /s/ as in *so,* you do not feel vibration of the vocal cords. When you say voiced sounds like /z/ as in *zoo,* you do feel vocal cord vibration.

SSSSSS

No vibration of the vocal cords.

ZZZZZZ

Vibration of the vocal cords.

EXERCISE 2   **A** 🔊 Listen to the eight consonant pairs. Do you hear the difference between the voiceless and voiced sounds? CD 4; Track 5

Voiceless	**Voiced**	**Voiceless**	**Voiced**
1. /p/ p̲ie	/b/ b̲uy	5. /θ/ th̲ank	/ð/ th̲ey
2. /t/ t̲own	/d/ d̲own	6. /s/ s̲ip	/z/ z̲ip
3. /k/ c̲old	/g/ g̲old	7. /ʃ/ sh̲ip	/ʒ/ ca̲sual
4. /f/ f̲ew	/v/ v̲iew	8. /tʃ/ ch̲eap	/dʒ/ j̲eep

B 🔊 Listen to the remaining consonant sounds. They are not paired.
CD 4; Track 6

Voiceless	**Voiced**
/h/ h̲at	/m/ su̲m, /n/ su̲n, /ŋ/ su̲ng, /r/ r̲at, /l/ l̲ap, /w/ w̲ell, /y/ y̲ell

C 🔊 Listen again to parts **A** and **B**. *Feel* the difference between the voiceless and voiced sounds. Put your hand on your throat and repeat the sounds and words.
CD 4; Tracks 5 and 6

DID YOU KNOW ?   Many students confuse voiceless and voiced consonant sounds.

My c̲lasses are great!   might sound like   *My g̲lasses are great!*

Airflow: *How does the air move?*

Stop Consonants

🔊 Listen and repeat these stop sounds.
CD 4; Track 7

/p/, /t/, /g/

Stop sounds are formed by stopping the air stream for an instant and then immediately releasing it. There are six English stop sounds: /p/, /b/, /t/, /d/, /k/, and /g/.

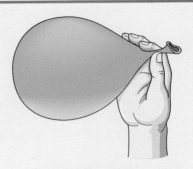

/t/ in *night* – the air flow stops

Continuant Consonants

🔊 Listen and repeat these continuant sounds. CD 4; Track 8

f-f-f, s-s-s, r-r-r

All sounds that are not stops are called *continuants.* Continuant sounds are formed by allowing the air to flow—or continue—out of the mouth. Some continuants, such as /r/, allow a lot of air to flow out. Others, such as /f/, limit the air flow; a continuant never stops the air completely, however.

/s/ in *nice* – the air flow continues

EXERCISE 3   **A** 🔊 Listen to the sounds and words. Notice the difference between stops and continuants. CD 4; Track 9

Continuant	Stop	Continuant	Stop
1. /v/ very	/b/ berry	5. /f/ laugh	/p/ lap
2. /w/ west	/b/ best	6. /s/ lice	/k/ like
3. /f/ fix	/p/ picks	7. /θ/ with	/t/ wit
4. /f/ four	/p/ pour	8. /z/ prize	/d/ pride

B 🔊 Listen again and repeat the sounds and words. CD 4; Track 10

EXERCISE 4   **A** 🔊 Listen to the speaker say one of the words or phrases in each pair. Check ✔ the word you hear. **CD 4; Track 11**

1. ___ less   ✔ let
2. ✔ bus   ___ but
3. ___ boss   ___ bought
4. ___ bath   ___ bat
5. ___ both   ___ boat
6. ___ a nice manager   ___ a night manager
7. ___ the rice soup   ___ the right soup
8. ___ he's gone   ___ he'd gone
9. ___ lost his prize   ___ lost his pride
10. ___ what size   ___ what side
11. ___ he plays piano   ___ he played piano
12. ___ ace something   ___ ate something

B 🔊 Check your answers with your class. Then listen to the speaker say both words or phrases in each pair. **CD 4; Track 12**

DID YOU KNOW ?   Students sometimes confuse continuants with stops.

Please pass the salt.   might sound like   *Please pat the salt.*

Place: *Where is the sound made?*

Both Lips: /p/, /b/, /m/

Say /p/, /b/, and /m/. The lips close and stop the air. For /p/ and /b/, air flows through the mouth. For /m/, it moves through the nose.

Say /w/. The lips are open and rounded. They let the air pass through.

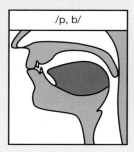
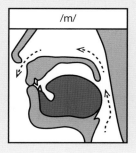
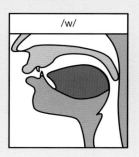

Bottom Lip and Top Teeth: /f, v/

Lightly bring the lower lip to the upper teeth. Force air through the light contact to say /f/. Add voice to say /v/.

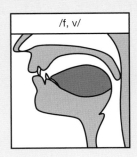

Tip of Tongue to Back of Upper Teeth: /θ, ð/

Loosely touch the tip of the tongue against the back of the upper teeth. Move air through the loose contact to say /θ/ as in *thank*. Add voice to say /ð/ as in *they*.

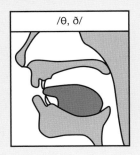

Tip of Tongue to Back of Gum Ridge: /t, d, n, l, s, z/

Feel the gum area behind the upper teeth. To say /t, d, n, l/, firmly touch the tongue tip against the gum ridge. To say /s/ and /z/, raise the tongue tip close to this gum ridge.

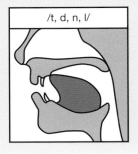

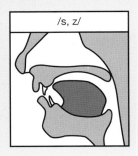

Tongue to Roof of Mouth: /ʃ, ʒ, r, y/

Move your tongue past the gum ridge to the roof of the mouth or palate. The front part is hard. To say /ʃ, ʒ, y/, the tongue is raised toward the hard palate. To say /r/, the tongue tip curls up.

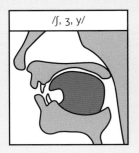

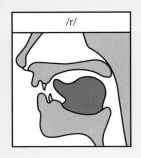

DID YOU KNOW ? The sound of *ch* in *cheese* combines /t/ with /ʃ/. The sound of *j* in *joke* combines /d/ with /ʒ/.

Tongue to Soft Palate: /k, g, ŋ/

Move your tongue further back. This part of the palate is soft. Say /k/, /g/, and /ŋ/, and feel the tongue on the soft palate. For /ŋ/, the air moves through the nose.

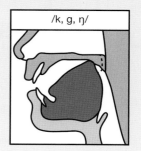

Air from Glottis: /h/

Take a deep breath. Release the air. The sound made when you release the air is /h/. Your tongue is in a resting position, and the sound is just a quick release of air from the vocal cords.

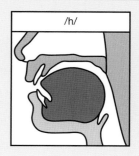

EXERCISE 5 **A** 🔊 Listen and repeat these common street names in the United States. Pay attention as you make each underlined sound. Circle the parts of your mouth that touch or almost touch. **CD 4; Track 13**

1. <u>M</u>ain	a. both lips	b. lips-teeth	c. tongue-teeth
2. <u>P</u>ark	a. both lips	b. lips-teeth	c. tongue-teeth
3. <u>F</u>irst	a. both lips	b. lips-teeth	c. tongue-teeth
4. <u>W</u>ashington	a. both lips	b. lips-teeth	c. tongue-teeth
5. Four<u>th</u>	a. both lips	b. lips-teeth	c. tongue-teeth
6. <u>L</u>ake	a. teeth-gum ridge	b. tongue-hard palate	c. tongue-soft palate
7. Pi<u>n</u>e	a. teeth-gum ridge	b. tongue-hard palate	c. tongue-soft palate
8. Oa<u>k</u>	a. teeth-gum ridge	b. tongue-hard palate	c. tongue-soft palate

(1. answer a. both lips is circled)

B 🔊 Check your answers with your class. Then listen again. **CD 4; Track 13**

C Name a street you know that starts with a consonant sound. _____

What sound is it? _____

What parts of the mouth touch or almost touch? _____

Sometimes students are not sure where to put their tongue and lips to make consonant sounds.

I took a ba<u>th</u>.   might sound like   *I took a ba<u>t</u>.*

9 Consonant Sounds and Spelling

OBJECTIVE
In this consonant lesson, you will learn about common sound-spelling relationships.

SUMMARY
English sounds are represented in writing in a variety of ways, often based on the origin of the word. Like vowels, consonants can also have more than one pronunciation. These words have the same first letter but different first sounds:

car /k/   cell phone /s/   good /g/   giant /dʒ/

Or they can have different first letters but the same first sound:

giant /dʒ/   juice /dʒ/   send /s/   city /s/

Some words sound exactly the same but have different spellings. These are called *homophones*.

threw, through   so, sew   know, no

Spelling Variations for Consonant Sounds

A Work with a partner. Complete the words in the sentences with the correct spelling of the consonant sound given.

1. /k/ I have a stomach a___ ___e. It hurts!

2. /z/ We are very bu___y. We have lots of work!

3. /s/ I lost my ___ell phone.

4. /g/ I saw a ___ ___ost on Halloween.

5. /n/ Do you ___ ___ow the answer?

6. /k/ We went for a swim in the la___e.

7. /ʃ/ I love swimming in the o___ean.

8. /s/ His major is ___ ___ychology.

9. /f/ First, write a rou___ ___ draft.

10. /s/ I love ___ ___ien___e class, but I don't like History.

Word Search								
s	e	p	b	g	h	o	s	s	u
b	u	s	y	i	s	p	l	j	i
d	e	y	d	r	c	e	l	l	g
e	u	c	l	t	i	z	h	b	n
r	o	h	i	v	e	k	w	u	a
o	u	o	k	k	n	o	w	z	c
u	l	l	e	w	c	o	l	y	h
g	h	o	s	t	e	w	a	q	e
h	g	g	u	k	b	y	k	m	w
z	l	y	b	r	o	c	e	a	n

B Find and circle the completed words from part **A** in the Word Search.

C Compare your answers with a partner. Student A, read the words that go left to right. Student B, read the words that go from top to bottom. Monitor your partner's pronunciation.

Homophones and -s Endings

A Work with a partner. Read the sentences and write the homophone with an -s ending for each word in parentheses.

1. (daze)   There are seven ____days____ in one week.

2. (dense)   Bob's not a good driver. His car has many _____ in it.

3. (Mrs.)   She _____ her son. He went away to college last month.

4. (ours)   My class is two _____ , from 8:00 to 10:00.

5. (raise)   The sun's _____ are bright today!

6. (weighs) There are two _____ to walk to my school.

7. (sense)   I have two dollars and twenty _____ .

8. (there's) This room is ours. That one is _____ .

B Find and circle the homophones from part **A** in the Word Search box.

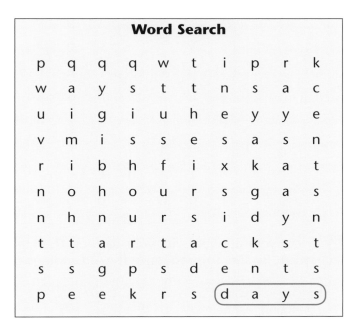

Word Search

p	q	q	q	w	t	i	p	r	k
w	a	y	s	t	t	n	s	a	c
u	i	g	i	u	h	e	y	y	e
v	m	i	s	s	e	s	a	s	n
r	i	b	h	f	i	x	k	a	t
n	o	h	o	u	r	s	g	a	s
n	h	n	u	r	s	i	d	y	n
t	t	a	r	t	a	c	k	s	t
s	s	g	p	s	d	e	n	t	s
p	e	e	k	r	s	⟨d	a	y	s⟩

C Check your answers in part **B** with your partner. Then say the sentences in part **A** with your partner. Be sure to pronounce the -s endings correctly.

> There are seven days in one week.

Homophones and -ed Endings

A Work with a partner. Read the words and write a homophone with an -ed ending for each. Then find and circle the words in the Word Search box.

1. board _____bored_____

2. disgust _____

3. find _____

4. guest _____

5. least _____

6. mind _____

7. mist _____

8. pact _____

9. past _____

10. road _____

Word Search

l	m	e	p	o	w	z	l	b
m	i	n	e	d	t	u	l	o
i	s	e	u	i	g	p	e	r
s	s	c	e	s	u	a	a	e
s	e	k	l	c	e	c	s	d
e	u	a	e	u	s	k	e	r
d	o	p	a	s	s	e	d	a
n	o	i	s	s	e	d	i	d
u	f	i	n	e	d	i	d	p
r	o	w	e	d	o	w	e	y

B Check your answers with your partner. Then take turns saying the homophones in part **A**. Be sure to pronounce the -ed endings correctly.

band, banned

MY **BAND**...   GOT **BANNED**.

10 What consonant sounds should you study?

OBJECTIVE

This page will help you identify some important consonant sounds to study.

SUMMARY

English consonant sounds that do not occur in your language or do not occur in the same places in words may be challenging for you to hear or say. The activity below will help you choose consonant sounds that you need to practice.

Selecting Consonant Sounds to Study

A 🔊 Listen to these sound pairs. If it is hard to hear the difference, one of the sounds may be difficult for you. Go to the consonant lesson for practice. **CD 4; Track 14**

1. /p/   mail the pills
   /b/   mail the bills   ☐ Easy ☐ Hard → *See Consonants 11, p. 154*

2. /t/   give me the time
   /d/   give me the dime   ☐ Easy ☐ Hard → *See Consonants 11, p. 154*

3. /n/   really done
   /m/   really dumb   ☐ Easy ☐ Hard → *See Consonants 12, p. 158*

4. /θ/   go to math
   /s/   go to mass   ☐ Easy ☐ Hard → *See Consonants 13, p. 162*

5. /ʃ/   cash it
   /tʃ/   catch it   ☐ Easy ☐ Hard → *See Consonants 14, p. 166*

6. /tʃ/   don't choke
   /dʒ/   don't joke   ☐ Easy ☐ Hard → *See Consonants 14, p. 166*

7. /l/   pilot software
   /r/   pirate software   ☐ Easy ☐ Hard → *See Consonants 15, p. 170*

8. /n/   a good night
   /l/   a good light   ☐ Easy ☐ Hard → *See Consonants 16, p. 174*

9. /b/   it's his best
   /v/   it's his vest   ☐ Easy ☐ Hard → *See Consonants 17, p. 177*

B Look at the Pronunciation Needs Form in Chapter 1 on page 5. Did your teacher note consonant sounds that were challenging for you to say? Write the sounds and one or two example words.

11 Initial /p/ _pie_ - /b/ _buy_; /t/ _time_ - /d/ _dime_; /k/ _cold_ - /g/ _gold_

OBJECTIVE
In this consonant lesson, you will learn to perceive and produce the voiceless and voiced stop consonants at the beginning of words and syllables.

SUMMARY
Making a clear distinction between voiceless and voiced sounds is important for clear speech, but this distinction in English is not easy for many students. _Stop_ sounds—/p/-/b/, /t/-/d/, /k/-/g/—are especially challenging. If speakers confuse related sounds, such as /p/ and /b/, then _"I ate the pear."_ could sound like _"I ate the bear."_

Notice

EXERCISE 1   **A** 🔊 Listen to the voiceless stops at the beginning of these words. CD 4; Track 15

1. /p/ pie   2. /t/ time   3. /k/ cold

B 🔊 Listen to the voiced stops at the beginning of these words. CD 4; Track 16

1. /b/ buy   2. /d/ dime   3. /g/ gold

C 🔊 Now listen to the voiceless–voiced word pairs. Do you notice a difference between the underlined sounds in each pair? CD 4; Track 17

1. pie - buy   2. time - dime   3. cold - gold

EXERCISE 2   **A** 🔊 Listen to the word pairs. CD 4; Track 18

1. pack - back   4. time - dime   7. coal - goal
2. peach - beach   5. tie - die   8. could - good
3. pear - bear   6. two - do   9. curl - girl

B 🔊 Listen to the word pairs. This time, some words are the same. If the words are the same (_pack - pack_), write S. If the words are different (_pack - back_), write D. CD 4; Track 19

1. _S_   4. ____   7. ____
2. ____   5. ____   8. ____
3. ____   6. ____   9. ____

C 🔊 Check your answers to part **B** with your class. Then listen again. CD 4; Track 19

Practice

Pronouncing Initial Voiceless and Voiced Stops

🔊 Listen to these word pairs. What signals the difference between voiceless and voiced consonants at the beginnings of words? CD 4; Track 20

Voiceless	Voiced
path	bath
time	dime
came	game

At the beginnings of words, voiceless consonants are pronounced with the sound of escaping air—called *aspiration*.

EXERCISE 3　　**A** 🔊 Listen to the word pairs from Exercise 2 again. Repeat each word pair. CD 4; Track 21

/p/ - /b/	/t/ - /d/	/k/ - /g/
pack - back	time - dime	coal - goal
peach - beach	tie - die	could - good
pear - bear	two - do	curl - girl

B Circle a, b, or c. Take turns reading the word pair you circled to a partner. Write the word pair your partner says. Do not let your partner see your book.

	Your Word Pairs		**Your Partner's Word Pairs**
1. a. peach - beach	b. beach - beach	c. peach - peach	_____ - _____
2. a. dime - time	b. time - time	c. dime - dime	_____ - _____
3. a. good - good	b. could - could	c. could - good	_____ - _____

C Check your answers with your partner. Then tell your class how you did.

TIP ▼ /p/, /t/, and /k/

When you say voiceless /p/, /t/, and /k/ at the beginning of words (*pair*, *turn*, *count*), hold a tissue in front of your mouth. You should release a puff of air. The puff of air or aspiration should make the tissue move. You can also hold your hand in front of your mouth. You should feel a puff of air.

EXERCISE 4 **A** 🔊 Listen to the speaker say sentence *a* or *b*. Check ✓ the matching response. **CD 4; Track 22**

1. a. This is a huge *p*ill. ✓ It's a vitamin.
   b. This is a huge *b*ill. _____ It's from the hospital.

2. a. Did he *p*ark? _____ Yes, in lot A.
   b. Did he *b*ark? _____ Yes, he saw a cat.

3. a. What's a good *t*ip? _____ 20 percent or more.
   b. What's a good *d*ip? _____ For vegetables or potato chips?

4. a. Is it *c*old? _____ No, it's warm and sunny.
   b. Is it *g*old? _____ No, it's silver.

B 🔊 Check your answers with your class. Then listen to the sentences and responses. **CD 4; Track 23**

C Work with a partner. Look at the sentences in part **A**. Student A, say sentence *a* or *b*. Student B, say the matching response. Then switch roles. Put your hand in front of your mouth to check for air on /p/, /t/, and /k/.

EXERCISE 5 **A** 🔊 Listen to the common words and phrases. **CD 4; Track 24**

1. *p*oor	4. *t*ell	7. *c*ause
*p*oor families	*t*ell a story	*c*ause trouble
in *p*oor health	*t*ell the truth	*c*ause accidents
2. *p*ositive	5. *t*en	8. *c*ost
*p*ositive attitude	*t*en minutes	total *c*ost
*p*ositive feedback	*t*en years	*c*ost per pound
3. *p*erson	6. *t*ake	9. *k*eep
every *p*erson	*t*ake off	*k*eep in touch
the first *p*erson	*t*ake advantage of	*k*eep trying

B 🔊 Listen again to part **A**, and repeat the words and phrases. Use a piece of paper or your hand to check for aspiration of the underlined sounds. **CD 4; Track 25**

EXERCISE 6   **A** 🔊 Listen to the paragraph. Notice the pronunciation of the underlined sounds in the highlighted words. **CD 4; Track 26**

> ## Tying the Knot: Who Pays?
>
> The <u>c</u>ost of an average wedding in 2014 was higher than ever before. One survey found that on average, a wedding costs 31,<u>2</u>13 dollars. Who <u>p</u>ays the bill? Well, traditionally, the bride's <u>p</u>arents <u>c</u>over most of the <u>c</u>osts. They <u>p</u>ay for the ceremony and the reception. The groom's parent's <u>p</u>ick up the cost of the dinner the night before. As costs climb, however, <u>c</u>ustoms are changing. <u>T</u>oday, 60 <u>p</u>ercent of <u>c</u>ouples pay some of their wedding costs. It is also becoming more <u>c</u>ommon for the bride's parents, the groom's parents, and the couple to divide costs equally.

B Work with a partner. Take turns saying each highlighted word from part **A**. Then listen again and read the paragraph out loud with the speaker. **CD 4; Track 26**

C Practice reading *Tying the Knot: Who Pays?* When you are ready, record yourself. Listen and monitor your pronunciation of the highlighted words, especially the words with /p/, /t/, and /k/. Re-record if necessary. Then submit your recording to your teacher.

📍 CHOOSE YOUR PATH

- For practice with stop consonant sounds at the *end* of words, see Chapter 4, page 23.
- For more practice with important consonant sounds, continue with the next lessons.

"I've fully costed my wedding plans, Daddy."

12 /m/ *so__me* - /n/ *su__n* - /ŋ/ *su__ng*

OBJECTIVE

In this consonant lesson, you will learn to perceive and produce /m/, /n/, and /ŋ/.

SUMMARY

Many students have difficulty hearing the distinction between /m/, /n/, and /ŋ/. These sounds are important because there are many words in English, such as *sum*, *sun*, and *sung*, that differ only by these sounds.

Notice

EXERCISE 1 🔊 Listen to the three sounds. CD 4; Track 27

/m/ ... /m/ ... /m/ ... /m/   /n/ ... /n/ ... /n/ ... /n/   /ŋ/ ... /ŋ/ ... /ŋ/ ... /ŋ/

EXERCISE 2 **A** 🔊 Listen to the word pairs. CD 4; Track 28

/m/ - /n/	**/m/ - /n/**	**/n/ - /ŋ/**
1. some - son	4. dumb - done	7. sun - sung
2. comb - cone	5. same - sane	8. thin - thing
3. warm - warn	6. game - gain	9. lawn - long

B 🔊 Listen to the word pairs. This time, some words are the same. If the words are the same (*some - some*), write *S*. If the words are different (*some - son*), write *D*. CD 4; Track 29

1. __S__	4. _____	7. _____
2. _____	5. _____	8. _____
3. _____	6. _____	9. _____

C 🔊 Check your answers to part **B** with your class. Then listen again. CD 4; Track 29

Pronouncing /m/, /n/, and /ŋ/

These three sounds are called *nasals*, meaning the air moves through the nose (not through the mouth).

/m/   The lips are closed. They keep the air from moving out of the mouth.

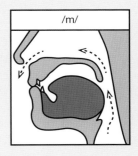

/n/   The lips are open. The front part of the tongue touches the gum ridge and keeps the air from moving out of the mouth.

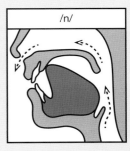

/ŋ/   The lips are open. The back part of the tongue touches the soft palate and keeps the air from moving out of the mouth.

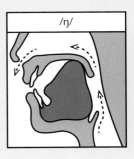

EXERCISE 3   🔊 Listen again. Repeat each of the three sounds after the speaker. CD 4; Track 30

/m/ ... /m/ ... /m/ ... /m/   /n/ ... /n/ ... /n/ ... /n/   /ŋ/ ... /ŋ/ ... /ŋ/ ... /ŋ/

EXERCISE 4   **A** 🔊 Listen to the word pairs again. Repeat each word pair. CD 4; Track 31

/m/ - /n/	/m/ - /n/	/n/ - /ŋ/
1. some - son	4. dumb - done	7. sun - sung
2. comb - cone	5. same - sane	8. thin - thing
3. warm - warn	6. game - gain	9. lawn - long

B Circle a, b, or c. Take turns reading the word pair you circled to a partner. Write the word pair your partner says. Do not let your partner see your book.

<table>
<tr><th colspan="3">Your Word Pairs</th><th>Your Partner's
Word Pairs</th></tr>
<tr><td>1. a. warm - warm</td><td>b. warn - warn</td><td>c. warm - warn</td><td>_____ - _____</td></tr>
<tr><td>2. a. gain - game</td><td>b. game - game</td><td>c. gain - gain</td><td>_____ - _____</td></tr>
<tr><td>3. a. sung - sung</td><td>b. sun - sun</td><td>c. sun - sung</td><td>_____ - _____</td></tr>
</table>

C Check your answers with your partner. Then tell your class how you did.

EXERCISE 5   **A** 🔊 Listen to the speaker say sentence *a* or *b*. Check ✔ the matching response. CD 4; Track 32

1. a. Do you want so**m**e?   _____ Yes, I love this candy.
   b. Do you want su**n**?   ✔ No, I'm already burned.

2. a. What's the li**m**e for?   _____ To put on your taco.
   b. What's the li**n**e for?   _____ To buy the latest smart phone.

3. a. This is Ti**m**.   _____ Hi Tim! Nice to meet you.
   b. This is ti**n**.   _____ Can we recycle it?

4. a. Is it a law**n** chair?   _____ No, it's for indoors.
   b. Is it a lo**ng** chair?   _____ No, it's pretty short.

B 🔊 Check your answers with your class. Then listen to the sentences and responses. CD 4; Track 33

C Work with a partner. Look at the sentences in part **A**. Student A, say sentence *a* or *b*. Student B, say the matching response. Then switch roles.

EXERCISE 6 **A** 🔊 Listen to the common words and phrases with /m/, /n/, and /ŋ/. Notice the sounds when alone and in phrases. **CD 4; Track 34**

1. war<u>m</u>
   war<u>m</u> weather
   war<u>m</u> welcome

2. sa<u>me</u>
   sa<u>me</u> day
   sa<u>me</u> time

3. ho<u>me</u>
   ho<u>me</u> office
   nursing ho<u>me</u>

4. su<u>n</u>
   su<u>n</u>set
   bright su<u>n</u>

5. rai<u>n</u>
   acid rai<u>n</u>
   pouring rai<u>n</u>

6. fi<u>ne</u>
   absolutely fi<u>ne</u>
   perfectly fi<u>ne</u>

7. somethi<u>ng</u>
   somethi<u>ng</u> like
   somethi<u>ng</u> else

8. ri<u>ng</u>
   weddi<u>ng</u> ri<u>ng</u>
   key ri<u>ng</u>

9. lo<u>ng</u>
   lo<u>ng</u> time
   lo<u>ng</u> hair

B 🔊 Listen again to part **A**, and repeat the words and phrases. **CD 4; Track 35**

EXERCISE 7 **A** 🔊 Underline the letters in the highlighted words that have the /m/, /n/, and /ŋ/ sounds. Then listen to the paragraph. **CD 4; Track 36**

Nine Lives

Some people say cats have nine lives. That is because many cats survive long falls. After they fall, they seem to return to life. Why? They turn in the air and land on all four paws. A study in New York found that cats were more likely to survive when they fell from seven to 32 floors than when they fell from two to six floors. That is because the cats had more time to spread their legs into an umbrella shape to slow down their fall.

"Yes, we will land on our feet … about half a mile down."

B 🔊 Work with a partner. Take turns saying the highlighted words in *Nine Lives*. Monitor your partner's pronunciation of the final /m/, /n/, or /ŋ/ sound. Then listen again and read the paragraph out loud with the speaker. **CD 4; Track 36**

C Practice reading *Nine Lives* with your partner or alone. When you are ready, record yourself. Listen and monitor your pronunciation of the highlighted words. Re-record if necessary. Then submit your recording to your teacher.

13 /θ/ _thing_ - /s/ _sing;_ /θ/ _thank_ - /t/ _tank_

OBJECTIVE

In this consonant lesson, you will learn to perceive and produce /θ/.

SUMMARY

Only a few languages have the voiceless /θ/ as in _thin_, so it is a difficult sound for most students. Many students replace /θ/ with /s/ (_sing_ for _thing_) or with /t/ (_tink_ for _think_).

Notice

EXERCISE 1 🔊 Listen to the three sounds. CD 4; Track 37

/θ/ ... /θ/ ... /θ/ ... /θ/   /s/ ... /s/ ... /s/ ... /s/   /t/ ... /t/ ... /t/ ... /t/

EXERCISE 2 **A** 🔊 Listen to the word pairs. CD 4; Track 38

/θ/ - /s/	/θ/ - /t/	/θ/ - /t/
1. think - sink	5. thank - tank	9. bath - bat
2. thing - sing	6. three - tree	10. both - boat
3. fourth - force	7. through - true	11. math - mat
4. mouth - mouse	8. thin - tin	12. tenth - tent

B 🔊 Listen to the word pairs. This time, some words are the same. If the words are the same (_think - think_), write S. If the words are different (_think - sink_), write D. CD 4; Track 39

1. _D_   5. ___   9. ___

2. ___   6. ___   10. ___

3. ___   7. ___   11. ___

4. ___   8. ___   12. ___

C 🔊 Check your answers to part **B** with your class. Then listen again. CD 4; Track 39

Pronouncing /θ/, /s/, and /t/

These three sounds are voiceless.

/θ/   Loosely touch the tip of the tongue against the back of the upper teeth, near the cutting edge. The tongue is flat. Force air through the loose contact.

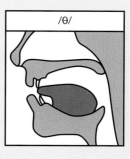

/s/   Point the front of the tongue close to the tooth ridge. The front of the tongue is in a narrow V-shape. Force air over the top of the tongue and make a hissing sound.

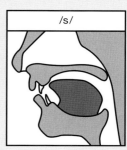

/t/   Touch the tip of the tongue against the gum ridge. Stop the airflow. Then release and let out a puff of air.

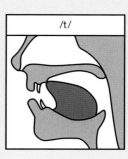

EXERCISE 3   🔊 Listen again. Repeat the three sounds after the speaker. CD 4; Track 40

/θ/ ... /θ/ ... /θ/ ... /θ/   /s/ ... /s/ ... /s/ ... /s/   /t/ ... /t/ ... /t/ ... /t/

EXERCISE 4   **A** 🔊 Listen to the word pairs again. Repeat each word pair. CD 4; Track 41

1. think - sink	5. thank - tank	9. bath - bat
2. thing - sing	6. three - tree	10. both - boat
3. fourth - force	7. through - true	11. math - mat
4. mouth - mouse	8. thin - tin	12. tenth - tent

B Circle a, b, or c. Take turns reading the word pair you circled to a partner. Write the word pair your partner says. Do not let your partner see your book.

Your Word Pairs   **Your Partner's Word Pairs**

1. a. sink - sink   b. think - sink   c. think - think   _____ - _____

2. a. fourth - force   b. fourth - fourth   c. force - force   _____ - _____

3. a. tank - tank   b. thank - thank   c. thank - tank   _____ - _____

4. a. mat - mat   b. math - math   c. math - mat   _____ - _____

C Check your answers with your partner. Then tell your class how you did.

EXERCISE 5   **A** 🔊 Listen to the speaker say sentence *a* or *b*. Check ✓ the matching response. CD 4; Track 42

1. a. Is he the fif<u>th</u> one?   ✓ No, the third one.
   b. Is he the fi<u>t</u> one?   ___ No, he's not in good shape.

2. a. Where's the pa<u>th</u>?   ___ Near the tree.
   b. Where's the pa<u>ss</u>?   ___ In the drawer.

3. a. Is it an eigh<u>th</u>?   ___ No, it's a fourth.
   b. Is it an a<u>ce</u>?   ___ No, it's a queen.

4. a. Is it <u>t</u>rue?   ___ No, it's false.
   b. Is it <u>th</u>rough?   ___ Not yet.

B 🔊 Check your answers with your class. Then listen to the sentences and responses. CD 4; Track 43

C Work with a partner. Look at the sentences in part **A**. Student A, say sentence *a* or *b*. Student B, say the matching response. Then switch roles.

EXERCISE 6 **A** 🔊 Listen to the common words and phrases with /θ/. Notice the underlined sounds when alone and in phrases. **CD 4; Track 44**

1. th<u>i</u>nk
   th<u>i</u>nk so
   th<u>i</u>nk about it

2. <u>th</u>ree
   <u>th</u>ree o'clock
   <u>th</u>ree times

3. <u>th</u>ird
   <u>th</u>ird world
   <u>th</u>ird floor

4. four<u>th</u>
   four<u>th</u> grade
   four<u>th</u> of July

5. <u>th</u>ousand
   <u>th</u>ousand pounds
   <u>th</u>ousand dollars

6. <u>Th</u>ursday
   <u>Th</u>ursday night
   <u>Th</u>ursday morning

7. me<u>th</u>od
   best me<u>th</u>od
   me<u>th</u>od of payment

8. fai<u>th</u>
   great fai<u>th</u>
   little fai<u>th</u>

B 🔊 Listen again to part **A**, and repeat the words and phrases. **CD 4; Track 45**

EXERCISE 7 **A** 🔊 Underline the /θ/ sound in the highlighted words. Then listen to the paragraph. **CD 4; Track 46**

Earth Day

Each year we celebrate Earth Day, and thousands of school children in Canada and the United States do what they can to protect and improve the environment. One year, students in Winnipeg started bringing trash-free lunches to school every day. Now they never throw anything away. Fourth-grade students in Texas raised more than one thousand dollars at a garage sale. They used the money to protect twenty-three acres of rainforest in Costa Rica. And students in Pennsylvania made cloth grocery bags for their parents to use year after year.

B 🔊 Work with a partner. Take turns saying the highlighted words in *Earth Day*. Monitor your partner's pronunciation of the /θ/ sound. Listen again and read *Earth Day* together with the speaker. **CD 4; Track 46**

C Practice reading *Earth Day* with your partner or alone. When you are ready, record yourself. Listen and monitor your pronunciation of the highlighted words. Re-record if necessary. Then submit your recording to your teacher.

14 /ʃ/ _sheep_ - /tʃ/ _cheap_ - /dʒ/ _jeep_

OBJECTIVE
In this consonant lesson, you will learn to perceive and produce /ʃ/, /tʃ/, and /dʒ/.

SUMMARY
Many students have difficulty hearing the distinction between /ʃ/, /tʃ/, and /dʒ/. They may say _see_ for _she_ or _cheap_ for _jeep_. These sounds are important because there are many pairs of words in English that differ only by these sounds.

Notice

EXERCISE 1 🔊 Listen to the three sounds. CD 4; Track 47

/ʃ/ ... /ʃ/ ... /ʃ/ ... /ʃ/   /tʃ/ ... /tʃ/ ... /tʃ/ ... /tʃ/   /dʒ/ ... /dʒ/ ... /dʒ/ ... /dʒ/

EXERCISE 2 **A** 🔊 Listen to the word pairs. CD 4; Track 48

/s/ - /ʃ/	/ʃ/ - /tʃ/	/tʃ/ - /dʒ/
1. see - she	5. she's - cheese	9. chin - gin
2. sue - shoe	6. sheet - cheat	10. chose - Joe's
3. so - show	7. wish - which	11. choke - joke
4. seat - sheet	8. wash - watch	12. rich - ridge

B 🔊 Listen to the word pairs from part **A**. This time, some words are the same. If the words are the same (_see - see_), write _S_. If the words are different (_see - she_), write _D_. CD 4; Track 49

1. _S_   5. ___   9. ___

2. ___   6. ___   10. ___

3. ___   7. ___   11. ___

4. ___   8. ___   12. ___

C 🔊 Check your answers to part **B** with your class. Then listen again. CD 4; Track 49

Practice

Pronouncing /ʃ/, /tʃ/, and /dʒ/

/ʃ/   Raise the front of the tongue toward the hard palate. Round the lips. Force air over the tongue. The tongue is relaxed. /ʃ/ is voiceless.

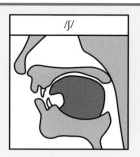

/tʃ/   Stop the air completely by making a stop /t/. Then open into a /ʃ/ sound. /tʃ/ is voiceless.

/dʒ/   Make the /dʒ/ exactly like the /tʃ/, except add voice.

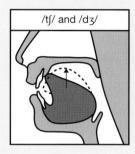

Note: /ʒ/ as in u*s*ually, plea*s*ure, A*s*ia, and deci*s*ion is made the same way as /ʃ/, but with voice. /ʒ/ is not as common as /ʃ/.

EXERCISE 3   🔊 Listen again. Repeat the three sounds after the speaker. **CD 4; Track 50**

/ʃ/ … /ʃ/ … /ʃ/ … /ʃ/   /tʃ/ … /tʃ/ … /tʃ/ … /tʃ/   /dʒ/ … /dʒ/ … /dʒ/ … /dʒ/

EXERCISE 4   **A** 🔊 Listen to the word pairs again. Repeat each word pair. **CD 4; Track 51**

/s/ - /ʃ/	/ʃ/ - /tʃ/	/tʃ/ - /dʒ/
1. <u>s</u>ee - <u>sh</u>e	5. <u>sh</u>e's - <u>ch</u>eese	9. <u>ch</u>in - <u>g</u>in
2. <u>s</u>ue - <u>sh</u>oe	6. <u>sh</u>eet - <u>ch</u>eat	10. <u>ch</u>ose - <u>J</u>oe's
3. <u>s</u>o - <u>sh</u>ow	7. wi<u>sh</u> - whi<u>ch</u>	11. <u>ch</u>oke - <u>j</u>oke
4. <u>s</u>eat - <u>sh</u>eet	8. wa<u>sh</u> - wat<u>ch</u>	12. ri<u>ch</u> - ri<u>dge</u>

B Circle a, b, or c. Take turns reading the word pair you circled to a partner. Write the word pair your partner says. Do not let your partner see your book.

	Your Word Pairs		**Your Partner's Word Pairs**
1. a. sheet - sheet	b. seat - seat	c. sheet - seat	_____ - _____
2. a. which - wish	b. wish - wish	c. which - which	_____ - _____
3. a. rich - rich	b. ridge - ridge	c. ridge - rich	_____ - _____

C Check your answers with your partner. Then tell your class how you did.

EXERCISE 5 **A** 🔊 Listen to the speaker say sentence *a* or *b*. Check ✔ the matching response. CD 4; Track 52

1. a. Did you get <u>s</u>eats?   _____ Yes, in the third row.

     b. Did you get <u>sh</u>eets?   ✔ Yes, I'll make the bed now.

2. a. What're you wa<u>sh</u>ing?   _____ My new shirts.

     b. What're you wa<u>tch</u>ing?   _____ A cooking show.

3. a. The <u>sh</u>ips are gone.   _____ They left the harbor.

     b. The <u>ch</u>ips are gone.   _____ We ate them.

4. a. Mar<u>ch</u> is almost here.   _____ Is it already the end of February?

     b. Mar<u>g</u>e is almost here.   _____ She just called on her cell phone.

5. a. Are you <u>ch</u>oking?   _____ No, I just have a cough.

     b. Are you <u>j</u>oking?   _____ No, I'm serious.

B 🔊 Check your answers with your class. Then listen to the sentences and responses. CD 4; Track 53

C Work with a partner. Look at the sentences in part **A**. Student A, say sentence *a* or *b*. Student B, say the matching response. Then switch roles.

EXERCISE 6 **A** 🔊 Listen to the common words and phrases with /ʃ/, /tʃ/, and /dʒ/. Notice the underlined sounds when alone and in phrases. CD 4; Track 54

1. <u>sh</u>ould   5. <u>ch</u>ild   9.   <u>J</u>une

   <u>sh</u>ould go   <u>ch</u>ild care   mid-<u>J</u>une

   <u>sh</u>ould be able   <u>ch</u>ild support   <u>J</u>une wedding

2.   <u>sh</u>ow   6.   <u>ch</u>ange   10.   <u>J</u>uly

   TV <u>sh</u>ow   address <u>ch</u>ange   end of <u>J</u>uly

   talk <u>sh</u>ow   political <u>ch</u>ange   4th of <u>J</u>uly

3. <u>sh</u>are   7. <u>ch</u>oose   11. chan<u>g</u>e

   <u>sh</u>are ideas   <u>ch</u>oose between   chan<u>g</u>e the subject

   <u>sh</u>are blame   <u>ch</u>oose whichever   chan<u>g</u>e your mind

4.   sta<u>ti</u>on   8. Fren<u>ch</u>   12.   a<u>g</u>e

   radio sta<u>ti</u>on   Fren<u>ch</u> language   school a<u>g</u>e

   gas sta<u>ti</u>on   Fren<u>ch</u> fries   middle a<u>g</u>e

B 🔊 Listen again to part **A**, and repeat the words and phrases. CD 4; Track 55

EXERCISE 7   **A** 🔊 Listen to the paragraph. Notice the pronunciation of the underlined sounds in the highlighted words. CD 4; Track 56

Take a Vacation!

Many workers in the United States are asking themselves a question: Why do I work so much? Americans get fewer vacation days than workers in most other nations. The average worker in the United States gets only ten vacation days a year, although after three or more years on the job, a worker may get more time. In China, workers are guaranteed 15 vacation days. Workers in Japan are guaranteed ten days, and usually take around 18. Danish and French workers are guaranteed 25 paid vacation days and take around 30. And oddly, even though Americans get fewer days, many don't even take all of them!

B Work with a partner. Take turns saying the highlighted words in *Take a Vacation!* Then write the rest of the words in the correct column.

/ʃ/	/tʃ/	/dʒ/
	question	

C Practice reading the paragraph with your partner or alone. When you are ready, record yourself. Listen and monitor your pronunciation of the highlighted words. Re-record if necessary. Then submit your recording to your teacher.

TIP ▼ Avoid adding sounds!

Read these sentences. Is there a difference in meaning?

They're going to change mail addresses.

They're going to change e-mail addresses.

Be careful not to add /iʸ/ to words that end in /ʃ/, /tʃ/, and /dʒ/. For example, say *page* (not *page-ee*). Say *match* (not *match-ee*). If you add a sound, you might change the meaning.

---

15 /l/ _light_ - /r/ _right_

OBJECTIVE
In this consonant lesson, you will learn to perceive and produce /l/ and /r/.

SUMMARY
Many students have difficulty hearing the distinction between /l/ and /r/. They may say _right_ for _light_ or _collect_ for _correct_. These sounds are important because there are many pairs of words in English that differ only by these sounds.

Notice

EXERCISE 1 🔊 Listen to the sounds. Notice the difference. CD 4; Track 57

/l/ … /r/ … /l/ … /r/ … /l/ … /r/ … /l/ … /r/

EXERCISE 2 **A** 🔊 Listen to the word pairs. CD 4; Track 58

1. light - right	4. lock - rock	7. collect - correct
2. long - wrong	5. load - road	8. alive - arrive
3. lead - read	6. lane - rain	9. play - pray

B 🔊 Listen to the word pairs. This time, some words are the same. If the words are the same (_light - light_), write _S_. If the words are different (_light - right_), write _D_. CD 4; Track 59

1. _D_   4. ___   7. ___

2. ___   5. ___   8. ___

3. ___   6. ___   9. ___

C 🔊 Check your answers to part **B** with your class. Then listen again. CD 4; Track 59

Pronouncing /l/ and /r/

/l/   Place the tip of the tongue against the tooth ridge. Air flows around the sides of the tongue.

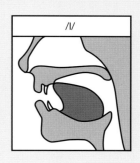

/r/   Curve the tip of the tongue back and up, but do not touch the roof of the mouth. The sides of the tongue touch the back teeth. The lips are slightly rounded.

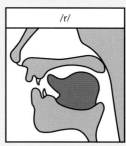

EXERCISE 3   Listen again. Repeat each sound after the speaker. **CD 4; Track 60**

/l/ … /r/ … /l/ … /r/ … /l/ … /r/ … /l/ … /r/

EXERCISE 4   **A**   Listen to the word pairs again. Repeat each word pair. **CD 4; Track 61**

1. light - right
2. long - wrong
3. lead - read
4. lock - rock
5. load - road
6. lane - rain
7. collect - correct
8. alive - arrive
9. play - pray

B   Circle a, b, or c. Take turns reading the word pair you circled to a partner. Write the word pair your partner says. Do not let your partner see your book.

	Your Word Pairs		**Your Partner's Word Pairs**
1. a. light - light	b. right - right	c. right - light	_____ - _____
2. a. read - read	b. lead - read	c. read - read	_____ - _____
3. a. rock - rock	b. lock - lock	c. rock - lock	_____ - _____
4. a. play - pray	b. play - play	c. pray - pray	_____ - _____

C   Check your answers with your partner. Then tell your class how you did.

EXERCISE 5 **A** 🔊 Listen to the speaker say sentence *a* or *b*. Check ✓ the matching response. CD 4; Track 62

1. a. Is it long?   ✓ No, it's short.

    b. Is it wrong?   _____ No, it's right.

2. a. Is it light?   _____ No, it's heavy.

    b. Is it right?   _____ No, it's wrong.

3. a. Did you collect them?   _____ No, they were a gift.

    b. Did you correct them?   _____ No, they're still wrong.

4. a. I have the lock.   _____ For the door?

    b. I have the rock.   _____ For your collection?

B 🔊 Check your answers with your class. Then listen to the sentences and responses. CD 4; Track 63

C Work with a partner. Look at the sentences in part **A**. Student A, say sentence *a* or *b*. Student B, say the matching response. Then switch roles.

EXERCISE 6 **A** 🔊 Listen to the common words and phrases. Notice the underlined sounds when alone and in phrases. CD 4; Track 64

1.   lot
       a lot of time
       a lot of money

2.   legal
       legal advice
       legal rights

3.   love
       love songs
       love story

4.   land
       owned the land
       bought the land

5. right
    right now
    right here

6. red
    red hair
    red meat

7.   road
    main road
    dirt road

8. rap
    rap music
    rap star

B 🔊 Listen again to part **A**, and repeat the words and phrases. CD 4; Track 65

EXERCISE 7 **A** 🔊 Listen to the paragraph. Notice the pronunciation of the /l/ and /r/ sounds in the highlighted words. CD 4; Track 66

Righty or Lefty?

One in every ten people is left-handed. But did you know that most left-handed people also favor their left ears, left eyes, and left feet as well? Left-handed people usually use their left eyes to look through a microscope. They lead with their left foot when walking. They wink more easily with their left eye. And their smile goes up more on the left side. The reverse is true for right-handed people. Which are you—a *righty* or a *lefty*?

B 🔊 Work with a partner. Take turns saying the highlighted words. Monitor your partner's pronunciation of the /l/ and /r/ sounds. Then listen again, and read the paragraph out loud with the speaker. CD 4; Track 66

C Practice reading *Righty or Lefty?* When you are ready, record yourself. Listen and monitor your pronunciation of the highlighted words. Re-record if necessary. Then submit your recording to your teacher.

"I had no idea you were upper-middle left tentacled."

16 /n/ _night_ - /l/ _light_

OBJECTIVE

In this consonant lesson, you will learn to perceive and produce /n/ and /l/.

SUMMARY

Some students have difficulty hearing the distinction between /n/ and /l/. They may say _night_ for _light_ or _ten_ for _tell_. These sounds are important because they are very common at the beginning, middle, and ends of words.

Notice

EXERCISE 1 🔊 Listen to the sounds. Notice the difference. **CD 4; Track 67**

/n/ … /l/ … /n/ … /l/ … /n/ … /l/ … /n/ … /l/

EXERCISE 2 **A** 🔊 Listen to the word pairs. **CD 4; Track 68**

1. night - light	4. news - lose	7. knock - lock
2. need - lead	5. not - lot	8. snow - slow
3. know - low	6. snap - slap	9. connect - collect

B 🔊 Listen to the word pairs. This time, some words are the same. If the words are the same (_night - night_), write _S_. If the words are different (_night - light_), write _D_. **CD 4; Track 69**

1. _S_	4. ___	7. ___
2. ___	5. ___	8. ___
3. ___	6. ___	9. ___

C 🔊 Check your answers to part **B** with your class. Then listen again. **CD 4; Track 69**

Practice

Pronouncing /n/ and /l/

/n/ The lips are open. The front part of the tongue touches the gum ridge and keeps air from moving out of the mouth. The air moves out of the nose.

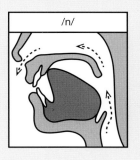

/l/ Place the tip of the tongue against the tooth ridge. Air flows around the sides of the tongue.

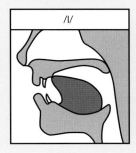

EXERCISE 3 🔊 Listen again. Repeat each sound after the speaker. CD 4; Track 70

/n/ … /l/ … /n/ … /l/ … /n/ … /l/ … /n/ … /l/

EXERCISE 4 **A** 🔊 Listen to the word pairs again. Repeat each word pair. CD 4; Track 71

1. night - light
2. need - lead
3. know - low
4. news - lose
5. not - lot
6. snap - slap
7. knock - lock
8. snow - slow
9. connect - collect

B Circle a, b, or c. Take turns reading the word pair you circled to a partner. Write the word pair your partner says. Do not let your partner see your book.

Your Word Pairs			Your Partner's Word Pairs
1. a. low - low	b. low - know	c. know - know	_____ - _____
2. a. lose - lose	b. news - news	c. news - lose	_____ - _____
3. a. knock - knock	b. lock - lock	c. knock - lock	_____ - _____
4. a. snow - slow	b. slow - slow	c. snow - snow	_____ - _____

C Check your answers with your partner. Then tell your class how you did.

/n/ night - /l/ light **175**

EXERCISE 5   **A** 🔊 Listen to the speaker say sentence *a* or *b*. Check ✓ the matching response.
CD 4; Track 72

1. a. Did you have a good night?   ___✓___ Yes, it was fun.

   b. Did you have a good light?   _____ No, I couldn't see.

2. a. Who needs the tour?   _____ All new employees.

   b. Who leads the tour?   _____ A guide.

3. a. It's a snow day.   _____ We expect a foot of snow.

   b. It's a slow day.   _____ Nothing is happening.

4. a. I connected them.   _____ To the Internet?

   b. I collected them.   _____ Where are they?

B 🔊 Check your answers with your class. Then listen to the sentences and responses. CD 4; Track 73

C Work with a partner. Look at the sentences in part **A**. Student A, say sentence *a* or *b*. Student B, say the matching response. Then switch roles.

EXERCISE 6   **A** 🔊 Listen to the paragraph. Notice the pronunciation of the /n/ and /l/ sounds in the highlighted words. CD 4; Track 74

New Year's Traditions Around the Globe

People love to celebrate the New Year. They make noise, eat food, and have fun. In China, they set off loud firecrackers to keep evil away. In North America, people blow horns. Sweet treats are common, too. For good luck, the Dutch eat doughnuts. The Irish eat a pastry called a *bannock*. And at midnight in Spain, people eat 12 grapes. In other places, the treats aren't as sweet. In India and Pakistan, people eat rice. In the Southern United States, they eat beans called black-eyed peas. How do you celebrate the New Year?

B 🔊 Work with a partner. Take turns saying the highlighted words. Monitor your partner's pronunciation of the /n/ and /l/ sounds. Then listen again and read the paragraph out loud with the speaker. CD 4; Track 74

C Practice reading the paragraph. When you are ready, record yourself. Listen and monitor your pronunciation of the highlighted words. Re-record if necessary. Then submit your recording to your teacher.

17 /b/ <u>b</u>erry - /v/ <u>v</u>ery

OBJECTIVE

In this consonant lesson, you will learn to perceive and produce /b/ and /v/.

SUMMARY

Many students have difficulty hearing and producing /v/. They may replace /v/ (*very*) with /b/ (*berry*).

Notice

EXERCISE 1   🔊 Listen to the sounds. Notice the difference. **CD 4; Track 75**

/b/ ... /v/ ... /b/ ... /v/ ... /b/ ... /v/ ... /b/ ... /v/

EXERCISE 2   **A** 🔊 Listen to the word pairs. **CD 4; Track 76**

1. ban - van	3. boat - vote	5. best - vest	7. cabs - calves
2. bet - vet	4. bent - vent	6. Barry - vary	8. carb - carve

B 🔊 Listen to the word pairs. This time, some words are the same. If the words are the same (*ban - ban*), write *S*. If the words are different (*ban - van*), write *D*.
CD 4; Track 77

1. <u>D</u>   3. ___   5. ___   7. ___

2. ___   4. ___   6. ___   8. ___

C 🔊 Check your answers to part **B** with your class. Then listen again. **CD 4; Track 77**

Pronouncing /b/ and /v/

/b/   Close the lips and stop the air stream.
Then release the air through the lips.
Add voice.

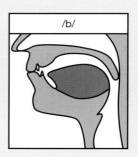

/v/   Touch the inside lower lip to the upper
front teeth. Direct the air stream through
the contact. Add voice.

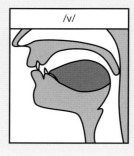

EXERCISE 3 🔊 Listen again. Repeat each sound after the speaker. CD 4; Track 78

/b/ ... /v/ ... /b/ ... /v/ ... /b/ ... /v/ ... /b/ ... /v/

EXERCISE 4 **A** 🔊 Listen to the word pairs again. Repeat each word pair. CD 4; Track 79

| 1. ban - van | 3. boat - vote | 5. best - vest | 7. cabs - calves |
| 2. bet - vet | 4. bent - vent | 6. Barry - vary | 8. carb - carve |

B Circle a, b, or c. Take turns reading the word pair you circled to a partner. Write the
word pair your partner says. Do not let your partner see your book.

<table>
<tr><td></td><td colspan="3" align="center">**Your Word Pairs**</td><td align="center">**Your Partner's
Word Pairs**</td></tr>
<tr><td>1. a. van - ban</td><td>b. ban - ban</td><td>c. van - van</td><td>_____ - _____</td></tr>
<tr><td>2. a. bent - bent</td><td>b. vent - vent</td><td>c. bent - vent</td><td>_____ - _____</td></tr>
<tr><td>3. a. best - vest</td><td>b. best - best</td><td>c. vest - vest</td><td>_____ - _____</td></tr>
<tr><td>4. a. carve - carve</td><td>b. carb - carb</td><td>c. carve - carb</td><td>_____ - _____</td></tr>
</table>

C Check your answers with your partner. Then tell your class how you did.

EXERCISE 5 **A** 🔊 Listen to the speaker say sentence *a* or *b*. Check ✓ the matching response. CD 4; Track 80

1. a. Did you sell your boat?   ✓ Yes, to my neighbor.

   b. Did you sell your vote?   ___ No! That's illegal!

2. a. Was that your best?   ___ No, I can do better.

   b. Was that your vest?   ___ No, mine is blue.

3. a. He owns some cabs.   ___ Oh, he must live in the city.

   b. He owns some calves.   ___ Oh, he must live on a farm.

4. a. What does *carb* mean?   ___ It's short for *carbohydrate*, or energy in your food.

   b. What does *carve* mean?   ___ It means to cut something, like meat.

B 🔊 Check your answers with your class. Then listen to the sentences and responses. CD 4; Track 81

C Work with a partner. Look at the sentences in part **A**. Student A, say sentence *a* or *b*. Student B, say the matching response. Then switch roles.

EXERCISE 6 **A** 🔊 Listen to the common words and phrases with /b/ and /v/. Notice the underlined sounds when alone and in phrases. CD 4; Track 82

1. <u>v</u>ote	4. <u>v</u>isit	7. fi<u>v</u>e
take a <u>v</u>ote	came to <u>v</u>isit	twenty-fi<u>v</u>e
<u>v</u>ote yes	a short <u>v</u>isit	fi<u>v</u>e percent
2. <u>v</u>iew	5. <u>v</u>ery	8. <u>b</u>ack
point of <u>v</u>iew	<u>v</u>ery interesting	come <u>b</u>ack
ocean <u>v</u>iew	thank you <u>v</u>ery much	<u>b</u>ack up
3. <u>v</u>oice	6. dri<u>v</u>e	9. jo<u>b</u>
<u>v</u>oicemail	hard dri<u>v</u>e	a great jo<u>b</u>
a loud <u>v</u>oice	dri<u>v</u>e home	jo<u>b</u> interview

B 🔊 Listen again to part **A**, and repeat the words and phrases. CD 4; Track 83

EXERCISE 7 **A** 🔊 Listen to the paragraph. Notice the pronunciation of the /b/ and /v/ sounds in the highlighted words. CD 4; Track 84

The Best Diet

Ben likes to eat a variety of foods. He doesn't believe in a certain diet. He's tired of hearing: "No-carbs!" or "Low-fat!" He knows it's best to eat healthy foods, like fruits, vegetables, and protein. He starts every day with a bowl of berries. He values his health, but he also really loves sweets. He sometimes eats a bit of chocolate or ice cream. "You have to live!" is his motto.

B 🔊 Work with a partner. Take turns saying the highlighted words. Monitor your partner's pronunciation of the /b/ and /v/ sounds. Then listen again, and read the paragraph out loud with the speaker. CD 4; Track 84

C Practice reading *The Best Diet*. When you are ready, record yourself. Listen and monitor your pronunciation of the highlighted words. Re-record if necessary. Then submit your recording to your teacher.

"Carb or non-carb section?"

WORD	PRONUNCIATION	TYPICAL PHRASE/SENTENCE
democratic	/ˌdɛ mə ˈkræ tɪk/	a democratic government

Most words in English (about 70 percent) take suffixes that do not change the stress of the base word.

1. Some of the more common suffixes that **do not** cause the stress to shift include the following.

-cy	**se**cret	→	**se**crecy
-er	**of**fice	→	**of**ficer
-ess	**host**	→	**host**ess
-ful	**mea**ning	→	**mea**ningful
-ish	**child**	→	**child**ish
-ism	**Bud**dha	→	**Bud**dhism
-ist	**stra**tegy	→	**stra**tegist
-less	**hu**mor	→	**hu**morless
-like	**life**	→	**life**like
-ly	**care**ful	→	**care**fully
-ment	in**vest**	→	in**vest**ment
-ness	**wil**ling	→	**wil**lingness
-or	co**or**dinate	→	co**or**dinator
-y	**wind**	→	**win**dy

Note this exception: Street names with the word *street* generally have strong stress on the first element: **Main** Street, **Peach**tree Street.

2. Some common suffixes that **do** cause the stress to shift include the following:
- The stress shifts to the syllable before these suffixes (and the first four account for almost 90 percent of all stress shifts):

-tion	**lo**cate	→	lo**ca**tion
-ity	**per**sonal	→	perso**na**lity
-ic	**al**lergy	→	al**ler**gic
-ical	**his**tory	→	his**to**rical
-ial	**me**mory	→	me**mo**rial
	benefit	→	bene**fi**cial
	essence	→	es**sen**tial
-ian	**Ca**nada	→	Ca**na**dian
	music	→	mu**si**cian
	Norway	→	Nor**we**gian
-ient	suf**fice**	→	suf**fi**cient
	nu**tri**tious	→	**nu**trient
-ious	**in**dustry	→	in**dus**trious
	suspect	→	sus**pi**cious
-eous	**cour**age	→	cou**ra**geous
-uous	ambi**gu**ity	→	am**bi**guous
-ify	**syl**lable	→	**syl**labify
-cracy	**de**mocrat	→	de**mo**cracy
-graphy	**pho**tograph	→	pho**to**graphy
-logy	**so**cial	→	soci**o**logy

- These suffixes are stressed:

-ee	**no**minate	→	nomi**nee**
-eer	**en**gine	→	engi**neer**
-ese	**Chi**na	→	Chi**nese**
-ette	ci**gar**	→	ciga**rette**
-esque	**sta**tue	→	statu**esque**
-ique	**tech**nical	→	tech**nique**

Index

Notes

Notes

Notes